Dedicated to those who have woken up,
looked in the mirror, and asked,
"Is this all there is?"

or, "Why must it be so difficult?"

or, "Now what?"

THE UNCOMFORTABLE ZONE

BREAKING THE BARRIER BETWEEN
YOU AND YOUR DREAMS

DON AWALT

The Uncomfortable Zone

Breaking the Barrier between You and Your Dreams

Copyright © 2018, Don Awalt

The views expressed by the author in reference to specific people in their book represent entirely their own individual opinions and are not in any way reflective of the views of Capucia, LLC. We assume no responsibility for errors, omissions, or contradictory interpretation of the subject matter herein.

Capucia, LLC does not warrant the performance, effectiveness, or applicability of any websites listed in or linked to this publication. The purchaser or reader of this publication assumes responsibility for the use of these materials and information. Capucia, LLC shall in no event be held liable to any party for any direct, indirect, punitive, special, incidental, or any other consequential damages arising directly or indirectly from any use of this material. Techniques and processes given in this book are not to be used in place of medical or other professional advice.

No part of this book may be reproduced or transmitted in any form, or by any means, electronic or mechanical, including photography, recording, or in any information storage or retrieval system without written permission from the author or publisher, except in the case of brief quotations embodied in articles and reviews.

Published by:
Capucia, LLC
211 Pauline Drive #513
York, PA 17402
www.capuciapublishing.com

ISBN: 978-1-945252-47-1
Library of Congress Control Number: 2018959037

Cover Design: Sumit Shringi
Layout: Ranilo Cabo
Editor and Proofreader: Gwen Hoffnagle
Book Midwife: Carrie Jareed

Printed in the United States of America

Table of Contents

An Uncomfortable Introduction 1

The Steps Not Taken 13

What Is Uncomfortable? 23

The Myth of the Comfort Zone 39

The Recipe of Life 53

Have Your Cake and Eat It Too 63

Know Your Fear, Know Your Truth 77

Pay Off the Debt on Your Life 85

Surrender or Give Up 93

You Are Okay 101

Hold On Tight 113

Change Your Story 123

What Is in the Way? 131

Step into the Zone 139

Acknowledgments 151

About the Author 153

An Uncomfortable Introduction

*Change the way you look at things,
and the things you look at change.*
– Dr. Wayne Dwyer

While I was writing this book and letting my friends know about it they would ask, "What is the book about?" At first I struggled to respond with a simple, succinct definition. I knew my intention was to share the secrets I discovered that have been leading me to create happiness and fulfillment in my life. Before this discovery I had been settling for less for most of my life, fearful of taking risks. And the risks I took often fell into disaster.

Yet I always dreamed of something better. There were things I wanted to do, places I wanted to go, and people I wanted to see. I wanted to take better care of myself and create more time to be of service to my community and the world at large.

THE UNCOMFORTABLE ZONE

I fell into a routine of playing it safe each day, hoping someday I would have the courage to do something new and different. Someday when I had more money. Someday when I had more time. Someday when I had new skills. Someday when the conditions were perfect to safely make some changes. Only then could I begin creating my dream life.

Someday never came.

Then, after way too many years, I was finally able to venture into the "Uncomfortable Zone." I changed my attitude and shifted the way I reacted to obstacles to the life I wanted. I no longer felt as though it was me against everyone and everything else. Life was looking up. I realized I had experienced a transformation. Never would I go back to letting feelings of discouragement confine me and make me want to just give up. I felt that if I could describe the bumpy and twisty process of my transformation, others could follow. I wanted to make it less difficult for others than it had been for me.

As I honed my message I found that my best response to someone asking about the book's purpose was to simply tell them the title and observe their reaction, which was usually one of intrigue as they reflected on what it is to be uncomfortable. I would then ask, "What does the Uncomfortable Zone mean to you?" Though responses varied, they all had one thing in common: each came with an emotional reaction. For many the term stirs a bit of fear that comes from feeling scared, anxious, inadequate, or overwhelmed when stepping out of their comfort zone to face a change. And it is that emotional reaction that much of this book is about.

AN UNCOMFORTABLE INTRODUCTION

The concepts in *The Uncomfortable Zone* are not new. They have been scribed by the greatest mentors and teachers throughout the history of civilization and are the topics of many books on the self-help and personal-development shelves at the bookstore. The teachings go back to the earliest manuscripts and scriptures penned by man. So why am I writing about them again?

I began studying personal development many years ago. I recognized early on that there were people who were living much better than I. More important, they were happy and I was not. I figured the reason they were happy was because they were successful. I set out to discover what success was and how I could attain it myself. I read countless books, took online classes, worked with coaches, attended personal-development seminars, and over three decades I had invested enough money in myself to have bought a modest home. Yet I was not getting the results I wanted. I was working the same job, was still troubled by my relationships, my health was deteriorating, and I was very dissatisfied. When I felt as though I was on the verge of creating something wonderful, another year would go by and I would find myself in pretty much the same place I had been. Many times I questioned the worth of pursuing greater things, having goals, and going after them. I found myself doubting it, joining the many who are skeptical about personal growth, and having regrets about the time and money I had spent.

The skeptic in me wondered, "If this information is the true key to success, then what am I missing? And why aren't more people successful?" And I asked, "Why is there so much material on the same topics?" I saw too that I was not alone. Others struggle with self-improvement, doing their best to be positive and take action on worthwhile goals, but getting very little in return. I truly wondered if along the way everyone had missed the very precise point upon which all success hinges. And I wondered if that is why the personal-development industry is a multibillion-dollar business and continuing to grow – that the secret to success had yet to be discovered.

In the early 2000s the Law of Attraction caught much attention. Soon everyone seemed to know what it meant even though the implied meaning wasn't always the same. I came to learn that the Law of Attraction meant that I was attracting what I was thinking about. My challenge was I could not sustain my focus on the things I wanted and instead went to my default way of thinking, which was that to get ahead I had to work hard, be competitive, promote my worthiness, and defend it. All the while I had to hide my shortcomings to avoid being judged.

I made many choices that were truly folly. Each disappointment led to another, shadowing all the wonderful blessings around me such that my focus was on the failures, not the successes. And that is why I saw little change in my life. I became lazy and did only that which was asked, no more. I was ashamed that I was not living up to the expectations that I wanted others to have of me. At times it was difficult to own that I was entirely responsible for what I created. It was easy to blame others and circumstances for my lack of success.

Even in my lowest times of doubt and insecurity I still felt there was something… something I was missing that could

AN UNCOMFORTABLE INTRODUCTION

create the life I desired – the ultimate key to success. After all, many successful people had all agreed that there is a formula. The same message is repeated so many ways. There is a simple recipe for having a rich, fulfilled, meaningful life. And by "rich" I am not referring only to money, although accumulated wealth can certainly be expected. I am referring to a life that is full of purpose such that each day is greeted with excitement and hope.

The point I was missing in my pursuit of success is that happiness does not come from success. It is the other way around. People who live happy, fulfilled, and grateful lives tend to be successful. Their lives may not be perfect, yet they are joyful in pursuing the lives they want to live on their terms by making simple daily practices habits.

Though there are some simple keys to being happy and successful, adopting them to change something for the better makes people uncomfortable. I spent much of my life standing at the edge, staring into a seemingly fearful zone of doubt and anxiety. I wanted something more out of life. I was not happy. Rather than doing something different, I chose to avoid my dissatisfaction, disappointment, discouragement, and frustration. I mastered suppressing my feelings. I achieved an emotionally neutral state: numb. Everything was okay. I was doing fine. Whenever I looked into the areas of my life that needed improvement, and there were many, I shied away to avoid facing my discontent. I remained in that state of denial, accepting what I had as enough and being grateful, all the while hiding from the regret I felt about many of my choices.

THE UNCOMFORTABLE ZONE

The first effective step I took to make a change in my life was simple, yet frightening: I had to accept that change was going to be uncomfortable. This meant leaving my safe and cozy neutral state and beginning to feel again – to get excited or frustrated; to have hope or despair; to celebrate others' wins or be jealous; to feel humble or proud. It was expressing feelings and experiencing them completely that would guide me through my fear. Feeling emotions again allowed me to identify the sources of the choices I had been making. By suppressing those feelings, I had had no idea what thoughts to challenge in order to think in a way that would help me create the life I desired; I only knew it wasn't working. I had stayed confined to my comfort zone, doing my best to keep my emotions neutral.

I wrote *The Uncomfortable Zone* to acknowledge my personal progress and give thanks to divine insight and conscious discipline to put it into words. I have learned that navigating into the Uncomfortable Zone is a choice to face my fears and create a life of joy rather than remain emotionally neutral, avoiding feelings of regret and doubt in myself. This resulted in many changes in my life, some as subtle as just being content with change; others have been quite profound.

The publication of this book is one example. I never realized the amount of work, discipline, and desire it takes to weave the thoughts in my mind into written words. I could easily have given up and quit, hoping someday I would have the time and energy to get it done. The first uncomfortable change I had to make was to accept that the book would never get done if I were to follow my old patterns; otherwise it would

AN UNCOMFORTABLE INTRODUCTION

have been done years ago. I had to make an investment in expert advice and trust that guidance. I also found it difficult to set my emotions aside and allow constructive criticism to be more "constructive" than "criticism." I had to face the reality that I was not managing my time well and that I tended to be disorganized in my thoughts and in my work. To get the book done I was going to have to shift my thinking from the chore of doing it to the benefits others could receive in the message. This journey has been the evidence of the power that lies in doing the uncomfortable tasks, accepting that I have room to grow and learn, being willing to change my attitude, and trusting that a positive transformation will result.

It took some time before I was applying these skills in my daily life. It took a while to believe that engaging my emotions to guide my thoughts would work. Yet I found that just about every successful person I know has done it the same way. They focus on being upbeat, supportive, energetic, and generally positive. When something bad happens, they experience their feelings about it, get over it, and continue on in a positive manner. It's easier to get through the tough times by embracing your feelings as normal, clearing your mind to think, and moving on.

I wrote this book with you in mind. When I look back I can see that all I knew was that I was not content; I did not realize how many things were not working in my life. I was complacent and simply accepting less than I knew I was capable of achieving. In my quiet times I wondered what I could do to start moving in a more uplifting direction, and discovered that I needed to let go of some things: what others thought of me, fear of failure, and modeling myself on others. I had to let go of my pride and adopt a new way of being proud of myself. I found that many others struggle with personal development, and the biggest challenge most have is that the changes they need to make are uncomfortable. They need what I found – an understanding that discomfort in doing something new is normal and a natural part of being human.

I get the impression from so many in the personal-development arena that they have arrived. They have created perfect lives for themselves. They gained experience and knowledge that is valuable to you, the reader. Their message seems to be that if they can do it, so can you. But what I have found is that these authors, speakers, and coaches know personal development is a continuous journey. They know and are willing to admit that there will always be improvements to make in their lives. There is a part of me that would love to boast of the wonderful things I have created in my life, especially those that have come from uncomfortable choices. I hesitate to share my low times because that might raise questions about my credibility to share what I have learned. In other words, I still struggle with what others think of me. Yet I talk to so many people who would like to know what I have learned and how to apply it in their own lives.

It has been a long journey for me to embrace this way of improving my life, but one that I have truly enjoyed and continue to enjoy. I recognize when I am uncomfortable facing a challenge, and ask myself why it is I am uncomfortable, which reveals how I think and releases the emotion so I can make a

AN UNCOMFORTABLE INTRODUCTION

conscious choice. I do not regret how long it has taken to learn this technique.

I have lived much of my life in frustration, fearful of taking chances and then regretting I had not taken them. Exploring why I am fearful and allowing myself to experience how I feel about that fear allows me to better make conscious choices and not be held hostage to beliefs based on past events. It is a process that takes consistent daily practice. When upset, frustrated, disappointed, or experiencing any feeling that stirs angst, I ask myself why I am feeling that way. The key to creating a life of fulfillment is to question what you are feeling and why you feel that way, and make choices that are not captive to that emotion.

Take a look at what is not working in your life. Take ownership of it as choices you and only you have made. That alone is your first step into the Uncomfortable Zone. Then be willing to explore and examine what you are feeling as being the result of what you are thinking. By thinking a different way, you will be in a position to make better choices.

In writing *The Uncomfortable Zone* I stand at the precipice of my own. There have been many starts and stops. Keeping the content simple and to the point has been a challenge. I often ask myself what credibility I have to write this book. Will anyone buy it? Will they read beyond this chapter? Or will it be another addition to the library of "shelf-help" books, never read and gathering dust? In writing it I knew I would need to expose why I have been disappointed in myself for so many years so that I could explain how I have turned my life in a positive direction, and it troubled me what others would think, especially those closest to me. With each doubt I am eased by asking myself, "Why am I thinking this way?" "Why is it I start and stop?" "Why is it I think the material is difficult to explain?" It is in answering these questions that I am able to understand my fears and why I have them, for these fears are reflections of much of my life. Though the fears are real, the reflections are imaginary.

Instead of talking about writing a book as I had for many years, I wrote it. In so doing I am disclosing many things about myself that conjure feelings of regret, disappointment, and remorse. I am reluctant to expose my inadequacies because it is not who I am now. And I am a bit embarrassed of my old behavior. If I had let those feelings continue to influence my decisions, this book would have never been written. I had to make different choices: to ask for help, mentorship, and professional editing; seek and find a publisher in alignment with my message; discipline myself to sit down and do the work; and trust the message would be delivered and received. And *The Uncomfortable Zone* is a wonderful reflection of how I now experience life. Instead of experiencing drudgery to get through each day, or being fearful of what others will think, it is a delightful experience to get to do what I want to do rather than something I have to do.

The journey from where you are to where you want to be brings you face to face with your Uncomfortable Zone. To make permanent changes in your life requires making changes from within, and that is going to stir up feelings that you would probably like to avoid. Understand that it does not have to be

AN UNCOMFORTABLE INTRODUCTION

difficult, to which I can personally attest. Many of my failures to get what I wanted in life resulted from perceiving this process as painful and tedious. I felt that I knew what I needed to know, and that was enough. It was not until I accepted that I needed to make changes in the way I thought and felt about my life that things started to get better. If there is but one thing I can convey to you in this book, I hope it is that the journey can be uplifting, joyful, and ever so rewarding. And it is certainly worth the effort.

It is my intention to give you the tools to make your changes more quickly than I did. The concept is quite simple to explain, but a bit complex to implement. To make a permanent change in your life, be willing to make permanent changes in the way you think and feel, and consciously make different choices. The process of doing so can be uncomfortable. Once you are comfortable with being uncomfortable, you are on the road to face your Uncomfortable Zone. And on the other side is the ideal life you wish to create.

I would like to share with you the moment when I realized that a change had occurred in my life – when I took ownership of my choices, without blame, without remorse, and accepted that I had been living life based on stories I made up about myself and the world around me. It was when I realized that I had just passed through a very uncomfortable period in my life and was about to face another. I had learned a major life lesson about making choices based on emotional reaction that usually resulted in little change. When a choice I made ended in failure, I realized that if I were to make a change in my life

I needed to make better choices. And those choices were only going to be possible when I could police my thoughts and confront the limiting beliefs that were holding me back. It was a time when all the things I had learned about personal development came together and led to the inspiration to write this book. I had made it through a troubling time, ready to start anew. The excitement of this opportunity brought with it doubt, uncertainty, and nervousness. I didn't know what I was going to do or how I was going to do it; I just knew that my life had taken a turn down a road I had never been on before.

The Steps Not Taken

If you always do what you always did, you will always get what you always got.
– Albert Einstein

I walked out of bankruptcy court, paused on the steps, and looked up into the sky. I felt naked, with everything stripped away. I was alone. I had no one to call. I felt hopeless, defeated, lonely... and simply drained. My biggest concern was not the lack of money, bank accounts, or credit, but how to keep this a secret. I was a fool to think that I could hide my pain. Those closest to me knew something was going on, but I had built up such a high wall of fear that it kept them out. Otherwise they might come to know the truth: that I wasn't the intelligent, confident, and successful person with tremendous potential they thought I was... or at least what *I thought they thought*.

But on that day I turned my gaze upward, peering through the tall buildings surrounding the courthouse. There was nowhere left to hide. It was a pleasant autumn day, with puffy clouds dotting a brilliant blue sky. The air was brisk. A few birds darted between the trees and buildings. In spite of what I'd just experienced, I took gratitude in the beauty around me. Frankly, it was all I could do because my mind could not grasp the magnitude of what had just happened. While part of me said, "All is in order; things happen for a reason," another voice was screaming, "You fool. You could have prevented this!" I was in a state where denial and reality met. In a solemn daze I thought, "Okay, that's behind me. *Now what?"*

This was not the most traumatic event of my life, and I know there are people who have been through far worse. But this blow took me down hard. I was nearly fifty years old, and now broke. My career was that of a financial advisor. I had dreams and aspirations of making a difference in the lives of others, and had been amply rewarded for my efforts. But I was living a delusional irony, advising others about money when I could not manage my own. I had stubbornly pursued this work, building my own business to prove to myself and others that I could make it work. It all crumbled around me as I came to accept that I was doing something that didn't really resonate with me. I quietly picked up the remaining pieces of my shattered life and hoped no one would find out about this appalling experience I'd just gone through.

In the difficult months that followed I was fortunate enough to return to a full-time job that paid very well and where my contribution was appreciated. It was there I stayed for quite a while, hiding in shame. I had to accept defeat, paying the bills that were not relieved by bankruptcy and managing to save a bit of money. But the steady paycheck and benefits I received were not fulfilling, and I had no idea what I was going to do next. I was very unsettled. And though I did my best to hide it, I was not happy.

I was standing at the border of what I came to call the Uncomfortable Zone, where the desire for something better is challenged by the doubt of ever having it. To create the life I desired I would have to enter and engage my fears. It was this event that made me realize I knew this place very well. In some form or another I had lived most of my life at the door to the Uncomfortable Zone, frozen in my steps, not satisfied but fearful of moving forward.

I am sure you know this feeling – imagining how nice it would be to make a change in your life and at the same time discouraged about what it will take to make it happen. It could be more money, a meaningful career, or working fewer hours. It could be better health, adhering to a diet and exercise – perhaps a better relationship with your significant someone or a family member. Or it could be that you want to do something that makes the world a better place. Whatever desire beckons you, there is a sense of danger in pursuing it. What if you fail or make a fool of yourself? What if you make a mistake or make some situation worse? What if the effort you make is just an embarrassing waste of time? You are blocked and unsure of what you should do, and in that confusion, do nothing.

In observing myself and others, it seems we yearn for a predictable life and a sense of stability. We go about our days repeating what we did the day before. Habits begin to form, and much of our lives go on autopilot. We have routines for getting dressed, going to work, eating meals, shopping, and how we interact with each other. Each day is replayed and it feels safe, secure, and comfortable. Even when vacations and special events are planned, those plans follow a sequence that is familiar. We want to live within parameters that feel safe.

I have also observed that it is not our inherent nature to stay in the same humdrum routine. We want to grow. We want to flourish. We each have desires that call to us. There is an old adage that the only thing constant is change. When called to make a change, it is uncomfortable. Our level of discomfort is based on two factors: how big the change is and whether or not we believe we can get through the change and retain our sanity. In other words, how risky it is for us. The riskier a change is, the more uncomfortable it is. The thought of it becomes a burden weighing us down with doubt that it is even possible. There is a certain point at which the scales of change tip into fear. Fear of the uncharted territory pushes us back to settle for less of a change – or to make no change at all.

What stands between – the chasm separating the security of stability from the desire to grow – is the Uncomfortable Zone. It often keeps us from creating the life we would love to live. I have wondered for years why many of us self-sabotage our efforts. We do *almost* what it takes to have the things we want, and then stop. It is as though we plow the field; sow the seeds; water, fertilize, and nurture them; watch them sprout; and just as they come to bear fruit, stand idly by as the sprouts wither and die.

Many of us become masters of excuses. We procrastinate on our dreams and pretend to be busy with a schedule full of activities, all in the name of being responsible adults – responsible to our families, jobs, and social agreements. There will always be another tomorrow when things are a little less busy, but today we have work to do and obligations to fulfill, and there are only so many hours in a day. The tomorrows string along like an endless chain, each day another link in the chain anchoring us to the only life we know.

What I have noticed is that this is how most of us live our lives. Unless we make a conscious effort to change, it is as though we are hardwired to live the life we have and nothing more. Each time we put forth the effort to make a change we are met with obstacles and challenges. Nothing comes easily. The effort just doesn't seem to be worth the struggle. Regret builds as the years pass. We want things to change but are overpowered by simply being satisfied with life as it is. It is as though it is our destiny to live a life of little meaning beyond that of the comfort of family and close friends. We fool ourselves into believing there is no need to change and that a life of liberty is just an unrealistic dream. Perhaps it is just our lot in life to do simple work and nothing more. We have much evidence to support that this is our destiny. Most efforts to change end in failure. It seems as though we can feel and act only one way, and that it is just the way we are. We come to accept it and that it is not possible to change.

I was haunted by the desire to reach out, inspire and lead others, and live a greater purpose. I experienced a great deal of personal development and growth working with mentors and professionals to understand why I was stuck. I wanted to know why I continued to repeat the same patterns in work, relationships, health, and service to a greater good. I knew that to create a richer, fuller life I needed to change. I wanted to know what was broken in me and how to fix it. I sought a magic formula – some secret recipe I could precisely follow to create the life I dreamed of.

And I found it. As a matter of fact, I found the secret repeated a number of times by many sources. It just finally began to sink in. To make a change in my life there was going to be a period of discomfort. This intimidated me. I convinced myself that it would be too much work. I believed it would require far more responsibility than I wanted to put forth. I believed the lie that I couldn't do it and that the effort would be futile. There was no possible way to have the lifestyle of liberty I desired, so why pursue it? Until I was able to confront those beliefs and the fears that bound me, little was going to change.

For much of my life I chose to stay in my comfort zone where I did not have to face the emotional struggles that come with life changes. To avoid pain I convinced myself that the home, career, relationships, and state of health I had were all good enough. I created a prison cell of made-up lies that locked me into complacency, settling for less than I deserved and not living the life I really wanted to live.

It was in this cell that I made my discovery: The concrete walls and steel bars were of my own making. It was going to take some work to break them down. This was tedious work for me because it was from the inside out. I had to look into my own life and discover why I had built these walls in which I was imprisoned. It meant I had to admit that the way I was thinking and the choices I was making were not in my best interest. My prison guard was my own underlying way of thinking – my subconscious mind. And because it was so clever and elusive, convincing it to leave me alone to deconstruct the cell was intimidating. This guard fed my ego. This guard looked after my safety, convincing me with evidence that I was safe and secure in my cell. To make a change in my life I would have to break down the beliefs I had adopted over time and take another approach to living my life. I had no idea what that entailed, and it frightened me.

As I struggled to discover what I was missing – why others seemed to enjoy the success that eluded me, I stumbled upon something that was more of a feeling than an answer. It wasn't easy to articulate what I had found. I really hadn't come upon anything new. There wasn't a secret lesson I discovered or a magic pill I took. It wasn't something in a particular book or something said by an inspirational speaker that turned me in the right direction. It was that moment on the steps of the courthouse when the question I asked took on a new meaning. The question was simply, *Now what*? It came from a different place in my heart than where my desperation and discouragement were lodged. I used to ask why things must be so difficult, why I just wasn't getting it, and why it seemed all forces were conspiring against me. But that day, when I really didn't think things could get any worse, I surrendered, and my query shifted. Instead of asking why life was such a struggle, I asked myself, *Why do you think it's such a struggle?*

Playing it safe may be easy but it creates stress when there is a desire for something better. It is easy to make up excuses and justify why making a change is too risky. It is easy to be complacent and pretend to be satisfied rather than take a risk on what you truly prefer. Yet those steps not taken – failing to take action on what you really want – eventually pave a path to one day saying, "I could have…, I would have…, I should have…, only if…" followed by a sigh of regret. Playing it safe is a threat to your dreams. This is not to suggest that you should take huge risks without some responsibility; instead, take a look at what is holding you back and why it seems scary. Face your Uncomfortable Zone and take a step in. You might fail. Your ego or reputation might get hurt. You might lose a little money. When compared to a life full of regret, self-doubt, and frustration, sometimes a little setback is a small price to pay.

Stepping into the Uncomfortable Zone is like entering a pitch black room looking for the light switch. You don't know if it is a pull string from the ceiling, a lamp, or a wall switch. There are obstacles in the room you cannot see. You don't even know if you are alone! Once you find the switch, everything in the room becomes quite clear. The fear is gone. The next time you find yourself in this dark room you remember where the light switch is and where some of the obstacles are. Each time it gets easier to shed light on the room. The first time in this zone seems daunting; but the more times you enter, the better equipped you are to find the switch and shed light on your surroundings. You must take that step in.

What Is Uncomfortable?

Do what you need to do, not what you want to do.
– Ida Keeling

What is the Uncomfortable Zone and why does it exist? Why does the thought of doing something new and different play out like a game of emotional ping pong, bouncing between your head and your heart? It is excitement battling fear, hope against doubt, self-confidence matched up with unworthiness. It shows up as an emotional swamp keeping you from the life you desire. It represents the reason you despise doing the little things you must do each day to have that life. It's breaking old habits and those old ways of reacting to things. It's the anxiety of not having enough time, money, health, love, patience, or just the mere determination to get through the ups and downs of doing something new. It's the struggle to stay focused on what you want and why you want it. It's the search for the courage to do the things that must be done, and mustering up the discipline to keep doing them. It can play out as jealousy regarding those who have already done it, judgment passed on their taking charge of their lives, deeply felt envy for their success, or despair in seeing them do it while you cannot.

You know when you are at the edge of this zone and not willing to go in. You don't want to accept anything less, yet you find yourself compromising on getting the very things you truly desire. You know what you need to do, yet you're not ready or willing to do it. You experience a flurry of excitement and hope, all the while biting your nails, wondering what horrible things might happen. Life circumstances come up out of nowhere and get in the way. It is almost as though you are sabotaged – betrayed by a universe you thought was supposed to come to your aid. Yet you know you must go on.

The Uncomfortable Zone has another face. It can also be when you know you are making the wrong choices yet you do everything you can to justify them. Despite your efforts, the chocolate cake wins over the apple. The snooze alarm is chosen over the gym. Money flies every direction but into savings. The same relationships come into your life as though they are waiting in line for their number to be called when the previous one has failed. Each new job is pretty much the same as the last, even when there were other careers you know you could have pursued. Just one more cigarette or one more drink won't hurt. When this sort of thing happens, it instills the belief that the effort is just not worth it, so why even try.

WHAT IS UNCOMFORTABLE?

Being uncomfortable is an experience created from thought. You form an intimidating image of what it would entail to make a change. You can identify the evidence that supports why it will be difficult. The discomfort you feel is founded on past experiences you have had, or witnessed others having, and your emotional reaction to them. You formed a belief about what is safe and what is not. When there is a perceived threat to your safety, whether physical or emotional, your focus is drawn to what could go wrong and how to combat it.

The battle is fought at the edge of this zone. It is not that you put up a fight when you voluntarily choose to embark on a change; when a plan is put together and acted upon it creates a sense of fulfillment – something is being accomplished and it feels good. It is more of an adventure, full of intrigue and hope for some favorable outcome. The intention is to make things better, and the steps being taken feel good. It might be a bit uncomfortable, yet the discomfort is within tolerable limits and manageable. Before you take action, the unfounded fear you have from past experiences can stop you in your tracks, clouding your vision of why it is you want to change.

In the context of doing something new and making a desirable change, the mass of reasons and excuses not to do it become bundled in a ball of fear. And the anxiety felt around that ball, pitted in your gut, is a defense against taking a step in. Whether action is taken or not depends on your tolerance of the discomfort being experienced, which comes from the *level of desire you have for the change*. When there is little need or desire to make a change, it is easy to shrug it off and forget about it. If, for example, you are offered a new job with better pay, yet you are perfectly happy at your present job, like your coworkers, feel valued, and prefer the location, you will probably stay rather than take the offer. If the conditions were reversed, and the new job paid less but offered better prospects for job satisfaction, you would probably give it strong consideration. This is where the discomfort appears. You ask yourself, "What if I'm making a mistake? Can I return to my old job if things don't work out? Is the company stable?" There are benefits in staying where you are and benefits in making the change. When the benefits of making the change outweigh the benefits of remaining complacent, change takes place. There is no perceived benefit in making a change without feeling a desire to do so.

When you decide to make a change, the people around you are either cheering you on or telling you that you are crazy and foolish for thinking you can be any better. You hear your inner voice join this chorus, arguing all the reasons to be content, satisfied that life is good enough as it is, and making up stories about what others would say. And yet another voice prods you to get up and go after something much better. You oscillate about which should get your ear. You fear to do what you know you must do. We each have our own version of this uncertainty.

You know what the Uncomfortable Zone is. It is when you experience what is uncomfortable to get what you want, before you even take the first step to getting it. The word *uncomfortable* is quite broad. What is uncomfortable for me might not be so for you. And what was uncomfortable yesterday might not be so today. Unless we confront this fear it keeps us from the joy and fulfilment we each deserve.

The Uncomfortable Zone does not magically provide what you want once you get beyond it. It can better be described as a brick wall. On its other side are all the worst-case scenarios and unknown challenges and dangers that are threats to your safety. Each brick represents self-designed beliefs about why getting through it is not worthy of the effort. You try to convince yourself that everything is fine where you are. You might have seen others make such attempts and fail, and you are not willing to experience the same pain. You might believe you are not worthy of what could be on the other side, or that you lack the experience or skill. The wall is built of your justifications for not going forward. Its purpose is to keep you safe and protect you from getting hurt. Getting past it looks intimidating and impossible.

I am reminded of my daughter who faced this wall when she stood at the turnstile to an amusement park roller coaster for the first time. Even though she had evidence that it could be fun – people exhilarated and laughing as they exited the ride – she was hesitant to go. She wanted to ride. It looked like it could be fun. Yet the high hills, steep turns, speed, noise, and everything else precarious about the roller coaster were bricks in her wall. Once in line, her mind flipped to and fro whether to go forth and ride or exit and go on another ride she already knew she would enjoy.

She persevered and we got on the ride together. As the coaster left the station and climbed the hill, I could see and sense her fear. The only thing to hold on to besides the handles in front of her was her trust in me. As we dropped into the hills and turns, the wind rushed across our faces. The rattling and shaking bellowed a deafening roar. She held on, fists clenched around the handles, sometimes with eyes open but mostly with them shut. Others screamed with exhilarated joy, but she barely uttered a sound. As the ride was coming to an end and we were coasting back into the station, I wondered if I had made a mistake and pushed her to do this before she was ready. Still shaking a bit from the raucous ride, I hesitated to ask her how she liked it.

As it turned out, she loved it! As she exited, her comment was something to the effect of, "That was fun!" followed with, "I want to ride it again!" And she immediately got back in line for a repeat ride. She ended up riding it quite a few times that day. Her challenge was not the ride itself; it was that first time in line, deciding whether she was going to go through with it or not. It was at the turnstile that she faced her fear, stepped through it, and strapped herself into the car. She had nothing to compare to the experience. Only in her mind was the impending thought that raised the anxiety, frightful anticipation, and sense of danger that beckoned her to get out of line and stay on the ground.

The roller-coaster example is commonly used to describe the ups and downs that can be experienced when doing something new, especially when the goal seems out of reach. More to the point of the Uncomfortable Zone is that choice to get on the ride. The reason something seems out of reach evolves over time.

WHAT IS UNCOMFORTABLE?

When setting out to do something new, it is an adventure full of hope and anticipation. Often things do not go as planned. Obstacles appear. Little setbacks become backed up to the point that you have to admit failure. Feelings get hurt. A reputation is damaged. Money runs out. It becomes exhausting to continue. So the only choice is to retreat to where you were. You are now equipped with an emotional experience to use as a defense for ever trying to do something new again.

When it is time to make a choice, to do something different, not knowing what the outcome will be or if it will last, a gap opens and is filled with all the reasons why the change is not a good idea. It can look like a maze. Along the way there are many dead ends. It's easy to become lost and confused. There could be dangers lurking around each corner to trip you, stemming from the pains and hurt you have experienced before. When disparaging thoughts overcome the desire to get through, the last hope is to retreat and limp back to where you started.

What's needed to find a route to the other side is a clear intent to find that safe passage, though it might take some trial and error. Holding dear to the rewards of an ideal intention is critical to making it through the challenges. The steadfast desire to succeed and make a difference in your life provides the patience to explore new choices, new ideas, and the attitude to persevere rather than give up. This does not mean the lines of the maze will be erased; turns and dead-ends are to be expected. There will be challenges, doubt, and confusion to discourage you. It is your intention to experience the feeling of success that provides the attitude to challenge the obstacles and make them opportunities. As you set out to do something new and different, the events that take place either guide you through the maze or act as defenses and push you back to where you began.

There are three defenses that appear when doing something new – something that is different enough that it is perceived as an imminent threat. These defenses are natural self-preservation mechanisms that are important for survival. They keep us safe and out of danger's way. It is important to accept these defenses as normal conditions of being human rather than as flaws that need mending.

There is the emotional defense that is the dramatic reaction to events as they take place. There is the conscious defense of analyzing an event and justifying it as a threat, then storing it away in the subconscious mind. And there is the metaphysical defense that can be described as resistance to change in nature. Together these three defenses battling against the intention to be successful create the discomfort and trepidation that comes with change. Each comes into play when setting out to do something new and different, and they work together to thwart any effort to make a change. This team of defenses is evidence that the body and mind are working as designed. They become automatic, engrained in our minds as habits. We do not have to think about what we need to do when our safety is threatened. We can simply react.

WHAT IS UNCOMFORTABLE?

Let's begin with the emotional defense. It's the easiest to identify because it usually shows up as fear. Fear is not a primary emotion, however. It is a reaction to something that is perceived to be a threat. The threat can be real, like an oncoming vehicle a little too close to the curb where you are standing. Or it can be imaginary, such as standing in line for an amusement park ride or asking the boss for a raise. Emotional feelings build and form the face of fear. The fear is real, not imaginary. What stimulates the emotions behind the fear might be imaginary. We often don't know what the outcome of something we have not tried will be. We make it up in advance based on past experience. Whether imaginary or real, the resultant emotional reaction is a natural response to the threat.

With fear being a reaction to a perceived threat, consider the word *perceived*. This is where thought comes into play – the mental defense, both conscious and subconscious, against doing something different. Your mind does not know the difference between what is imaginary and what is true fact. You can close your eyes and imagine a past event – whether hilarious, calm and soothing, or painful – and experience that same emotion as though the event were occurring now. The emotion you experience when facing something that feels uncomfortable is based on past experiences and your memories of them. Sometimes the past experience is not remembered, yet it is there, buried deep and influencing your reaction to doing something different. Just the anticipation of an experience being uncomfortable can result in fear.

THE UNCOMFORTABLE ZONE

There is interplay between the emotions you feel and what you think. There are both conscious and subconscious choices you make to avoid stirring up past emotions. Using reason and logic you come up with a list of all the reasons to choose one way or the other. The diet would be too restrictive, the gym too expensive. The new career will take time away from the family. There is no point working on the relationship because nothing is going to change until the other person changes. You form rigid examples of what is right and what is wrong based on events you remember and the emotional reactions you had to them. Over time your choices are logged away in your subconscious mind as habitual behavior. You don't have to think about them anymore. When your conscious mind perceives a threat, your subconscious mind reacts in a pre-orchestrated way, with you as the conductor. An emotion is stirred and a choice is made to avoid getting hurt, even though it is nothing more than a perceived threat. Nothing has happened to justify a threat. You only think it will.

This mental defense is responsible for many unconscious choices you make. These mental workings are responsible for learning to walk, to speak, and to interact safely in your environment. You learn from events and experiences and form a mental picture of how to avoid getting hurt, both physically and emotionally. Most of the choices you make each day are without thought, and are made to minimize the emotional impact of experiencing an event. Your subconscious mind works on autopilot.

WHAT IS UNCOMFORTABLE?

Emotional and mental defenses team up and over time create a physical neural network that resides in your brain and throughout your nervous system. Your reactions to events, and how you interact with the world around you, form a life story you live out each day. This story resides in your nervous system. Neural pathways are formed into a web that defines your personality. The strands of this web are coated and protected with a substance called myelin, which also accelerates transmissions within the network. The primary purpose of this neural network is to ensure your safety and survival. It is where you learn not to touch the hot stove or stand in front of the oncoming bus. Yet it continues to form and mature and then identify what is a threat and what is not. When an event happens, you react based on this learned behavior. If you have ever thought that you are hardwired to think a certain way, you are correct. The good news is that this neural network can be rerouted – it is just part of the discomfort of making a change. Here's what Dr. Joe Dispenza said about this wiring in the movie *What the #$*! Do We Know!?*:

> Nerve cells that fire together wire together. If you practice something over and over again those nerve cells have a long-term relationship. If you get angry on a daily basis, get frustrated on a daily basis, if you suffer on a daily basis, if you give reason for the victimization in your life, you are rewiring and reintegrating your own net on a daily basis and that neuro net now has a

long-term relationship with all those other nerve cells called an identity. We also know that nerve cells that don't fire together no longer fire together. They lose their long-term relationship. Because every time we interrupt the thought process that produces a chemical response in the body, every time we interrupt it, those nerve cells that are connected to each other start breaking the long-term relationship.

When we start interrupting and observing, not by stimulus and response and that automatic reaction, but by observing the effects it takes, then we are no longer the body-mind conscious emotional person that's responding to its environment as if it is automatic.

Emotional and mental defenses work together in the physical body to form protective behavior, providing the responses needed to any threat, real or perceived. As mentioned earlier, they are a team. These empirical defenses pull us away from anything that could cause us harm. In working together, they are a predefined program that has been developed over time through life experience. The result is that the choices you make and the actions you take are either in alignment with your past experiences, which is comfortable, or in opposition, doing something different, which is uncomfortable.

It might seem that once this programming is in place there is no hope for change. Quite the contrary; the program can be altered. As Dr. Dispenza mentioned, "when we start interrupting and observing" we can break the servitude we have to this conditioning. It takes consistent and deliberate effort to recognize that the result in our lives was created by the emotional and mental reactions we had to events. We then need to accept that we created a neural network that expresses itself as our routine behavior, or habits. When we are able to recognize the patterns, interrupt them, and make a separate choice, the pattern can be altered and a new program written.

You can probably relate to how the emotional and mental defenses work together in remembering life events – good, like grandma pulling freshly baked cookies out of the oven; or bad, like the playground bully who wouldn't leave you alone. There was an event, and there was an emotional reaction to it, forming a belief. Choices and actions followed based on this belief until the neural net was formed. It then became a habit.

The third defense mechanism to making a change is not as easily identified or explained. The metaphysical defense differs from the emotional and mental defenses in that it is an energetic force that exists among all living things. For the force of life to exist, flourish, and grow, this contrary force must push back, resist, and create decay. It is this resistant force that manifests as the emotional and mental defenses against change. It is evidence that we are subject to the same physical laws of nature as the rest of creation.

Everything in nature begins as an energy force, has a period of growth to maturity, and then decays. The force pushing against growth creates strength. It provides a necessary resistance, just as exercising with weights does. Take the resistance away and the strength soon slips into weakness. The force of growth pushing against decay prolongs existence and creates stamina. By nurturing a sapling and giving it fertile soil and the right amount of water and sunlight, it can grow into a mighty tree, living for many years. But not without a struggle. The sapling must endure times of cold, harsh winds, disease, draught, and deluge. It must be able to tolerate the unpredictable conditions in the spot where it chose to grow, expand, flourish, and prosper. The resistance is there to give the tree strength and endurance. When the tree submits to resistance, it dies.

Think of your dreams as this sapling. The two forces of growth and decay interact in a game in which one is always winning over the other. And this game plays out in each of us each day. Either we are growing and expanding, or we are decaying and contracting. When embarking on a change, this resistant force guides the emotional and mental defenses to hesitate in taking action. It stirs the feeling of despair, anxiety, and frustration, doing what it can to protect you or to force you to ask a simple question: "Is it really worth the effort?"

Have you ever wondered why things must be difficult? Why it must be such a challenge to get the things you want in life and that seem just out of reach? These discouraging feelings either build stamina and resilience or create a state of depression and wanting to give up on your dreams. It is up to you to decide. By nurturing and caring for the force of growth in order to be happy, flourish, and prosper, you can always overcome the resisting force. The fertile soil, water, and sunlight come in the form of motivation, inspiration, and purpose. It answers the

WHAT IS UNCOMFORTABLE?

question of whether it is worth it.

The emotional and mental defenses are the human form of this metaphysical power of resistance. This power builds strength and a resilient character. It gives you stamina and the perseverance you need to take on difficult tasks. When you cower to resistance, you lose confidence; become indecisive, exhausted, and weak; and perhaps even become ill. The metaphysical powers of growth and decay are always present. It is up to you to choose how you apply your mental and emotional faculties when obstacles are in the way of your dreams.

The title of this chapter is "What Is Uncomfortable?" It is as much a statement as it is a question. The discomfort in making a change is a personal experience. It is for you to identify what is uncomfortable. When the desire to do something new confronts your habitual behavior, your Uncomfortable Zone is created. Your discomfort provides the key to understanding how you think and the choices you make. Your emotional energy about making a change clouds your ability to think, but you must step in and experience the emotion of why change is uncomfortable, and experience it completely. This defuses the emotion, allowing you to think clearly.

The emotion you feel when making a change that seems frightening is normal and shows that you are in perfect working order. The thoughts that bounce around in your head between your dream and all the reasons it is out of reach are part of an elaborate system of neurology and chemistry designed to keep you safe. Thought, emotion, and action work together, and they are always working together in the choices you make. Emotion is the evidence of how you think. And it is emotion that drives habitual choice. To make different choices in order to make a change in your life, explore not only what is uncomfortable to you, but also why it is uncomfortable. Your answer identifies the boundary of your zone and is the key to experiencing the emotion you feel about doing something new, behaving in a different way, adopting a new attitude, and how you live your life.

The Myth of the Comfort Zone

There are risks and costs to a program of action. But they are far less than the long-range risks and costs of comfortable inaction.
– John F. Kennedy

As I came upon the concept of the Uncomfortable Zone and decided to use it for my book's title, it begged a discussion about its logical counterpart. In my research on the origin of the term *comfort zone* I found that it cannot be traced to a single author, speaker, or any other source. Most definitions suggest that it is a familiar state or level where one feels safe and at ease. In hearing how the term is used by others, this seems to be the essence of what they describe: a safe place, familiar, with little threat.

Comfort zone is such a common term that its meaning is assumed, yet it is unique to each of us. For some it is a place to be confident. It can be a place to retreat to and recuperate when things are a bit scary. Some use it to hide or avoid the burden of living up to others' expectations. We have different kinds of comfort zones for the different areas of our lives: money and career, health and fitness, and relationships; and internal, emotional comfort zones for the love we have for ourselves and for others. Because we are each unique, it's a bit complex to define. So commonplace is the term *comfort zone*, yet so individual the meaning.

There is one common element of the comfort zone that we all share. It is predictable. Or at least we feel it is predictable. Surprises are few, far between, and minor. Risk is low and well managed. As a seed of corn is properly placed in the soil, watered, nurtured, and eventually a corn stalk sprouts forth, it is a safe state in which the effort put forth produces expected results. Choices made and actions taken are in alignment with the beliefs we have about ourselves and the world around us. Our tools, skills, and abilities are enough to get by. While in the comfort zone, tomorrow will be much as yesterday. Anything outside of it feels threatening.

The reason the comfort zone is unique to each of us is that it is created through our interpretation of life events. We all start off with core values that define what is good and what is bad, and the difference between right and wrong. Through these core values we construct our comfort zones. That which is good and right is comfortable and that which is not is uncomfortable. Our values are engrained in us at a very early age, mostly coming from our families and those closest to us. As babies we were dependent on those caring for us to survive, and it was from them we learned how to survive on our own. Early on, we had no other influence.

From these values we adopted as babies, we formed beliefs about who we are. With each life event we assessed what we believed to be true. We constantly asked ourselves, "Do I believe I am a good person, or bad, or sometimes good and sometimes bad? Am I quick to learn, or need more time? Am I outgoing and popular, or more inward and intimate? Am I willing to take chances, or am I cautious?"

We also formed beliefs about the world and those around us by asking, "Do I believe others are friendly, loving, and trustworthy, or are they indifferent, uncaring, and competitive? Is the world a place of bountiful abundance, or is it limited, with some having much more than others?" Our individual life experiences fostered countless such questions, stirring our individual thoughts. It is through these many questions and our responses that our beliefs were formed about who we are and the world in which we live.

We applied this myriad of beliefs to the different parts of our lives: how we learned in school, how we interacted with others, how we took care of our bodies, and eventually how we earned a living and fit into society. Through life experiences we formed beliefs about who we are and our capabilities and limitations. When we live within the realm of those capabilities and limitations, we feel we are in our comfort zone.

Through these beliefs about who we are and where we fit in, we make choices. Often there is little thought in the choices we make; they just seem to be the right thing to do at the time.

And when we do make a conscious effort to think something through, the foundation we most often depend on is that of our beliefs that have formed over time.

Have you ever wondered why the same things keep happening to you? When you change jobs do you realize that it is the same job, just a different employer? Do the same people keep showing up in your relationships? Perhaps you have come into a nice sum of money, only to see it gone in a short period of time. Or you have gone on a diet and quickly found those lost pounds. Your beliefs form a "life map" which your thoughts naturally follow. Just like roads on a map, there are routes you habitually take to get to the destination of being comfortable and safe and avoiding conflict. You don't have to think about much when you follow the known routes. This is your default way of thinking, and it creates your attitude – that is, how you show up to others. You make choices based on your default thinking. And the actions you take create the results that make up your life. This default way of thinking – your life map – grew naturally over time from the seeds of your early childhood values.

To illustrate the power of this default way of thinking, reflect back on this morning. Did you consciously choose to get yourself ready for the day? When you brushed your teeth, which hand held the brush and which held the tube of toothpaste? When you put on your shoes, was it sock-sock, shoe-shoe, or was it sock-shoe on one foot then the other? Which foot do you start with, right or left? Did you brew your morning beverage but don't even remember doing it? These defaults govern most repetitive tasks you do each day. The mind is marvelous and efficient in how it delegates methodic duties to the subconscious. We all have default actions we take, their foundations in learned behavior. That learned behavior is the way you think.

When you feel stuck, and life isn't moving forward, it's your thoughts driving your behavior that have you in a rut. You are doing your best to make better choices, yet it is your mind that is governing the outcome. The choices you make follow the map that your subconscious beliefs dictate.

Following this habitual pattern creates a cycle. It begins with what you believe about yourself and the world. Over time you delegate much of your thought to your subconscious mind, resulting in habitual behavior. As others say and do things that stir your emotions, or unpredictable events happen and things just aren't going your way, your reaction is automatic – there isn't a point of conscious thought between the event and how you react. The choices you then make are just as predicable, following the familiar routes on your life map. Unless there is a conscious choice to take another route, the results of your actions follow the old pattern. Your mind is doing all it can to create conditions that support what you believe to be true, but it's like missing an exit on the highway because you are following your familiar route. The results you get are in perfect alignment with your beliefs unless there is a conscious choice to take that exit out of the cycle.

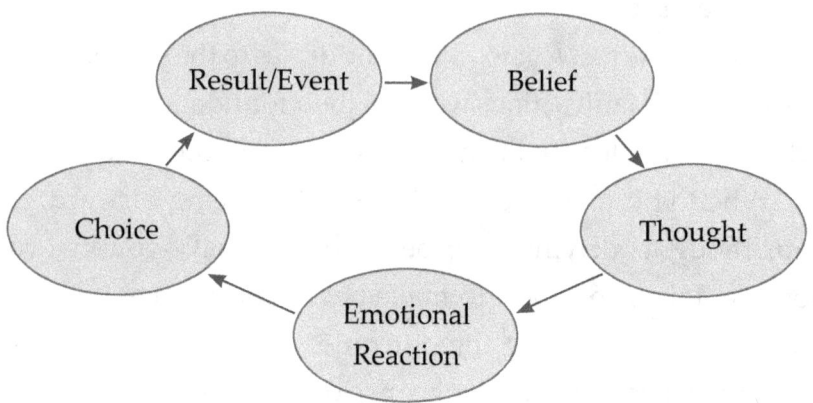

This cycle of belief to thought, to emotional reaction, to choice, to result or event, and back to belief is your comfort zone. *When the results you get in life support your beliefs, you are in your comfort zone.* Even if you hate it. The results are predictable. There is no challenge to the way you think or what you believe. The choices you make and the actions you take are well known. And they are *predictable*.

There really is no such thing as the comfort zone. It is simply a state in which behavior is effortless, surprises are few, and the only changes that take place are by mere chance. The way the term is most often used is to describe operating in such a way that is not uncomfortable. A better description is that it is a complacent and predictable zone where risk is minimized. Granted there are times when things are going well, you feel on top of the world with all in order, and it feels comfortable. But this is not a sustainable state. At some point the power of growth beckons you to expand with new desires, and the power of resistance pulls back. It is at that point that the short-lived zone of comfort is dissolved. Unless you face the fearful emotions head-on and pursue your new dreams, the only choice remaining is to be complacent and satisfied with what you currently have.

As commonplace as the term *comfort zone* is the concept of "getting outside the comfort zone." It is usually used in reference to making some sort of change – stretching a bit, taking a chance, changing an attitude, or forming a new habit. Getting out of your comfort zone is a voluntary risk to do something differently. It is risky because there is an increased chance of failure. Getting out of your comfort zone happens in one of two ways: either something happens in your life that is outside the formula – that is, you got an unpredictable result; or you consciously begin to make choices that challenge your thoughts and what you believe.

A simple test is to imagine how it would feel to switch hands with the toothbrush and the tube of toothpaste, or to switch to sock-shoe, sock-shoe instead of sock-sock, shoe-shoe. When you begin to examine your habitual behavior throughout the day, you notice a pattern. You follow familiar routes on your map. Your conscious mind has been busy for years delegating tasks to your subconscious mind and it has done so in a deliberate, systematic manner. The way you interact with others, your attitude, the choices you make, and how you go about accomplishing tasks all follow a pattern. As long as you operate in this predefined pattern, everything seems normal and predictable. You are operating in your comfort zone. When you begin to see the pattern you can then make different choices. Making a conscious choice that challenges your old pattern can feel odd, and depending on the perceived risk, it can feel frighteningly uncomfortable.

Switching things up is uncomfortable because you increase the risk of failure. We are taught that failing is not a good thing. The most formidable years of your life were in school when you learned much more than the academic protocol. One big lesson was that doing things correctly is expected. Doing them wrong was called out and had bad consequences. When a quiz was graded, where was the focus – on the correct answers or the mistakes? You were brainwashed to believe that failure is always bad. Whenever the risk of failure presents itself, in any form, it can feel uncomfortable.

The Uncomfortable Zone is not simply getting out of your comfort zone, though doing so is certainly uncomfortable. When doing something new, it does not take long before that also becomes comfortable. Your comfort zone expands with new experiences and how you feel about them. The Uncomfortable Zone is created when something happens that challenges just how comfortable it is to remain in the comfort zone. It could be as dramatic as losing a job, a divorce, a frightening health condition, or a disastrous event; or it could be something quite subtle like telling someone the tag of their blouse is hanging out. It could be that what we call a comfort zone – going about each day with little risk – just wears away over time. We get bored and want to make some changes. The old comfort zone erodes and an expanded one is created. The old safe, familiar, predictable, low-risk attitudes and activities are no longer acceptable.

But the Uncomfortable Zone will always be there. When the chocolate cake wins over the apple, when you choose the old job over the new career, when you avoid the difficult conversation, there is no comfort zone to return to. There is no longer a warm, cozy, safe enclave where you feel no guilt. The best you can find is a complacent zone where you simply settle for what you had, even if you don't like it.

It is in this settling-for-less zone where your resistance to a positive change in your life outweighs your desire to have it. Change takes place only when the benefits of having a better life outweigh the benefits of being complacent. Adopting a new way of thinking to live a new life is an uncomfortable process. And reverting to the comfortable when your heart tells you it can be better is uncomfortable as well. Safe and predictable are no longer acceptable, yet the steps to do something new appear frightening and precarious. You've created a wall founded in fear. On one side life may be predictable but not acceptable. On the other are the doubtful and skeptical feelings that anything better is possible. It is only by making a conscious choice to examine your emotions, adopt a new attitude, and make new choices that you overcome this fear.

A comfort zone is nothing more than a state of mind. It is not real. It is a perception in which the results you get, the people you meet, bad luck or good, are all predictable according to your belief of yourself and the world around you. Living in your comfort zone does not mean you are at bliss. It only means that life is going as you expect it. When you have decided the results you are getting are no longer acceptable, you form a new perception of what is comfortable, make a choice to do something new, and what seemed to be comfortable before becomes less so. Your so-called comfort zone continues to contract into a state of living safe and tossing away your dreams. Because your comfort zone is only a state of mind, it is constantly changing. As I wrote earlier, what was comfortable yesterday may no longer be comfortable today. It can be changed at will by simply taking a step and doing something that at first seemed uncomfortable, and not being frightened away by the emotion, thought, and obstacle at play to keep you where you are.

This is the time to make different choices. There are a couple of ways to do this. The quickest way is to adopt an empowering attitude that creates new feelings, uplifting and hopeful. It is a constant effort to assess and monitor the attitude you are now expressing. By consciously choosing to feel better, there is a gradual change in belief. It is also fragile, because if you have an underlying belief that you are not good enough or that you are plagued by bad luck, it is easy to slip back into your old ways. It takes discipline to constantly monitor your attitude, yet it is effective. Associate with people who think the way you would like to think. Study their behavior, their attitudes. Use them as role models, learning to act and speak the way they do. Notice how they go about their day, their mannerisms, and habits. By observing, your conscious mind is delegating tasks to your subconscious mind. At night before retiring into sleep, reflect on your day. What could you have done better? If you were to relive some of the scenes that took place, how could you have responded better? How would your respected role models have responded?

Be careful not to beat yourself up with self-judgment. The life map you have created up to this point is the result of your mind working perfectly as designed. It has done its best to create habits and behaviors that protect you from being hurt, both physically and emotionally. Just imagine that if your mind has been so effective in creating who you now are, it must be just as capable of creating new ways of thinking, new behavior, and new habits.

Another strategy is to directly go after the belief that holds you back. If you believe you are unskilled, don't have enough money, or are burdened with obligations, such beliefs are restricting you. They can be changed, which is a more direct and permanent approach, yet it is not as easy as simply changing your attitude. A good personal-development coach can help you identify the programs that are driving your behavior and uncover new ways of thinking that support you. One of the most difficult things about personal development is you are living in your drama. It is difficult to recognize because you are operating within the programs you naturally created to keep yourself safe and secure. You meet any threat to this programed way of living with resistance. It stirs emotion, resulting in fear. Your conscious mind justifies your behavior. It takes a skilled observer to see your behavior and help you draw out the beliefs that are driving it.

A coach can help you identify your cycle of thought to behavior to the results you create. Selecting someone who can help you adopt new habits is the most frightening step for most people. The thought of someone who could actually help make a positive difference in your life threatens the programming that has successfully gotten you to where you are.

Another direct approach to modifying your limiting beliefs is through meditation and visualization. Take time each day to close your eyes and let your imagination roam. What could your life be like if there were no limitations? At first you will probably be plagued by the things in your life you don't want – the bills, the dead-end job, ill health, abusive relationships. When such thoughts enter your mind, imagine them dissolved away and replaced by the life you do want. Then it is very important to feel the joy in having that life. Feel it so deeply that it makes your spine tingle. Doing this exercise daily sends new instructions to your subconscious mind where your habits are formed. Over time there will be changes in what you believe, the thoughts that dominate your mind, your behavior, and the choices you make. All will start coming into alignment with these new beliefs.

Many give up meditation and visualization practices soon after beginning them. The restrictive defenses mentioned in the prior chapter are always pushing you back into your old programmed way of thinking. It does take discipline, and it helps to associate with others who do the same. Having support from others who are also determined to improve their lives is very helpful when you're falling back into your old ways. Learning this approach is uncomfortable because it's outside your normal and predictable way of living, and anytime you challenge your automatic behavior your natural defenses step in to push you back into your imaginary comfort zone.

Here is another though to ponder: Is it possible to be comfortable being uncomfortable? The answer is yes! When I say that the term *comfort zone* is a myth, I am referring to the cycle of engrained beliefs driving action to create results that support the engrained belief. The cycle is predictable. It has low risk. It is not uncomfortable. It is at best only complacent. I see many examples of people living their lives in this cycle, and they are very dissatisfied. They may be comfortable, yet there are desires that seem out of their reach. Likewise there are those who challenge this cycle. These are the goal-driven, self-motivated people who embrace making improvements in their lives. In challenging their beliefs they know there are risks. There will be setbacks. They might fail, only to try again. But they are comfortable with taking these chances. In other words, they are comfortable being uncomfortable.

Many of the successful people I admire understand the importance of doing uncomfortable tasks and having a good attitude while doing them. I long wondered how they could have the difficult conversations, make the challenging decisions, and be disciplined in all they did. It seemed that in their success they discovered how to operate in spite of their fears. I wanted to know their secret, and I found it.

The Recipe of Life

If you don't like something, change it.
If you can't change it, change your attitude.
– Maya Angelou

In line with the Uncomfortable Zone, getting outside of the comfort zone, and the behaviors and patterns we form to get through the day, I would like to share with you the recipe of life. It would seem that having such a recipe would be all that is needed. This book would end here, and there would be no reason to read any other or to do further study. Mastering this recipe would be all it would take. Everything you desire in life would magically manifest and that would be it.

The ingredients are well known:
- Know what you want
- Believe you can have it
- Trust it will all work out
- Do something

This isn't my recipe. It has been around for a long time. The ingredients are concepts that are not new. As I mentioned before, countless books have been written about them. This recipe is simple – so precise and predictable that most take it for granted. But it's not a step-by-step process. Approaching it as such is what causes many to struggle, attempting to master each ingredient in turn. As with any recipe, there are instructions for how to combine them. These are fairly simple as well:

- Combine the four ingredients in even portions.
- Continue to combine them consistently and repeatedly over time.
- Check for doneness by paying attention to what is happening and how you feel about it.

THE RECIPE OF LIFE

It is this last step – checking for doneness – that brings the recipe together. You pause and examine all the things that make up your life: your health, job, money, relationships – *everything*, and the result is your version of the recipe. How you feel about it dictates whether you will change something or stay the same.

The recipe is so precise. And each of us uses it every day. Everything in life, everything you experience, is the result of this recipe. The part I failed to understand for many years is that it creates failure as well as it does success. I think this bears repeating:

This recipe produces a life of frustration, poverty, illness, and misery just as well as it produces happiness, wealth, health, and fulfillment.

Once I grasped that it was just as effective at creating havoc in my life as it was harmony, all I had to do was take a look at the ingredients I was using and the way I was combining them.

It would be easy to argue that no one wants a shallow or abusive relationship. Nor do they want ill health, obesity, or a dead-end job working for an over-demanding boss. Nobody wants a meaningless life, devoid of hope and in a state of despair, or with ever-increasing debt and unexpected expenses fueling it. It doesn't matter that you consciously want the opposite of these; if they currently exist in your life, they are what you are creating. And this recipe is why.

Because whatever our lives look like is indeed what we unconsciously want, believe, trust to be true, and create. This is as true for dismay as it is for harmony. There are benefits to creating a life of discord, such as getting sympathetic attention from others and getting support for your belief that the world is out to get you and no one is to be trusted. Perhaps you are jealous of others' success and it feeds your jealousy. It's important to recognize *and accept* that you created the condition you do not like. Assess how you feel about it and why. Then take a look at the underlying need you are satisfying. In other words, understand what it is you *really* want.

As an example of identifying the underlying need to be filled, a client of mine found herself in a pattern of attracting partners who at first seemed perfect. A relationship would start out well, with lots of fun and all the signs of being everything she wanted. A year would go by and the bliss would begin to fade. Eventually arguing would ensue and she found herself being blamed for all that went wrong. As she exited the relationship to end the emotional abuse, there was a network of dear friends to catch her, console her, and tell her how much she was loved and deserving of someone who truly appreciated her. This same scenario played out in her life in many ways; not only in her intimate relationships but in business relationships as well. She always had a support circle in place to catch her when she fell. I had to ask her, "What is more important to you: a fulfilling, steadfast relationship built on communication and cooperation, or the support of your dear friends who are there to lift you when you're down?" Her response led me to think about many of the choices I make in my own life. "I want both," she said. Why was it I thought one must be more important than the other? One of her needs was already met: her support network of friends. A sacrifice is not always necessary to manifest what we want.

There are times when the first ingredient – what you really want – is only what you believe you deserve or *can* have – the second ingredient. The things that happen each day – the rude driver, the unexpected tax bill, friends who let you down, losing your job – are all events you expect to be in alignment with your bad luck. This is what you trust will happen. It all works out, even though you may not like it. And the choices you make and actions you take are in alignment with that recipe. You have combined these ingredients equally and consistently over time. When you check for doneness you either like, dislike, or are indifferent to what you have created.

I like to use the example of baking a chocolate cake, yet all you have is a recipe for lasagna. And lasagna is the only thing you know how to bake. You have been making it for years and have mastered the recipe. When you set out to bake the cake without a proper recipe, you are guessing at best. Knowing the lasagna always comes out great, you set the intention of having chocolate cake, yet default to the instructions for lasagna. As it is baking, you know it smells like lasagna, and certainly not like cake, but you trust the recipe, as it has never failed. When the timer signals that the cooking time is complete, to your dismay lasagna comes out of the oven. Frustrated, you return to the recipe, attempting to substitute ingredients to create a chocolate cake. The result is horrible, nothing but chaos and a messy kitchen. At some point you give up, claiming chocolate cake is not possible for you. Others may be able to do it, but not you.

It might sound preposterous that all you need is the proper recipe and a little practice to pull a perfect cake out of the oven. Well, the same holds true for the things in your life you wish to change. The difference is that the right recipe is not quite as easy to come by as one for chocolate cake. You first have to recognize and accept that the strategy needed to make a change in your life is the same one you used to create the mess you already have.

This concept was as hard for me to swallow as a cake baked with a lasagna recipe. It is the key to understanding how change takes place. It was when I realized that it was only me who could take responsibility for my life that things began to change. When I blamed others or some unfortunate circumstance for something I did not like, I hadn't taken ownership of my part in it. Did I want to go bankrupt? Did I want the revolving door of relationships? Did I want to be lethargic, out of energy, and overweight? As crazy as it might sound, the answer is *yes*. It certainly was not my intention to create those conditions; I was not out to consciously create a miserable life. Yet the ingredients were there. It was the life I believed I could have, and each day I went about the motions of creating it, trusting that it would happen. It was my default way of operating – my lasagna, so to speak. I evenly combined my vision of what life could be, my belief in it, my level of trust, and my daily actions. I did this repeatedly over time.

THE RECIPE OF LIFE

And each day I wallowed in frustration and hopelessness that I couldn't do anything to change it.

Using the example above, if you want chocolate cake you need a good chocolate cake recipe and you must adjust the ingredients *as a group*. To make a positive change in your life, you must first be very clear about what it is you really want – what the recipe is for – and why you want it. You must also believe it is possible. You must trust that the conditions and resources to make the change will be available to you. And you must take action on those opportunities. The error often made is to focus on changing just one of the ingredients, such as what you want – the goal. If you don't *believe* you deserve it or can have it, it's like substituting an ingredient in the recipe. No matter your goal, you must believe you can achieve it and trust it will work out. Then with some action in alignment with that desire, miracles can happen when you trust they will.

Many people feel frustrated and defeated when they do not meet their goals or when an action they take ends in failure, and they give up on their dreams and never try again. They return to their old way of thinking, now with supporting evidence that the effort is just not worth it. This is the time to instead examine your feelings about the result created. Was it a failure or just a learning experience? Why did it stir up so much emotion? Learn to accept the result as being based on old programming, and take responsibility for both the program and the choices you made. Let yourself feel the emotions brought on by the failure. By owning them and exploring them you diffuse them. Once the emotions are gone, a shift takes place, and your conscious, rational thought now has a chance to choose a different way to act.

The trick is finding the right ingredients for the changes you wish to create in your life. What I have found to be the best source is the people you look up to and respect. Paying attention to how they act, how they react, what they do, and the nuance in how they do it is invaluable. They know how to *bake the cake*. Most people who have it together are ready and willing to share what they think about, which provides clues for how to think productively. One common characteristic is they study personal development. They practice it. They apply the life recipe and pay close attention to the results and how they feel about them. Do they get upset when things do not go as planned? Usually yes. Do they dwell on it? Usually no.

The reason there is so much material available on personal development is because this concept has proven to be flawless through the ages. Each person who discovered it wanted to write about it, and many did. The recipe works, but you have to keep evaluating your results and tweaking your mix of ingredients. This is why the personal-development industry continues to thrive. If there were a program, book, or mentor that was 100 percent effective, that would be it – we would just have to do those exercises and *voilà!* – life would be perfect. Yet because we are unique we must each find our own key to happiness and satisfaction with life.

You are responsible for everything in your life. You created it. Even if this angers you, I am only sharing what has been discovered by countless others before me. It's a tough concept to accept, which is why it has been written about for centuries. But if it's true that you created *this* life – the life you are now living, imagine the power you have to create something else!

To know what you want, *and* believe you can have it, *and* trust that everything will fall into place is quite a bit to grasp. Then to repeatedly apply the recipe evenly and consistently over time, checking in with your results and your feelings, requires much discipline and support. It is much easier to have doubt, question the simplicity of the recipe, and do nothing. To apply the recipe means to do things differently, check your attitude regularly, and admit things to yourself that your ego might not be ready to accept. If you are not happy with something, change it. If you cannot change it, change your attitude about it.

Have Your Cake and Eat It Too

*Experience is not what happens to a man;
it's what a man does with what happens to him.*
– Aldous Huxley

The quality of a cake depends on the recipe, the ingredients, the tools, and the expertise in following the recipe. The instructions in the prior chapter are precise. They work every time. Know what you want. Believe you can have it. Trust it will all work out. And do something. Combine these four ingredients together in equal proportions. Continue to stir consistently and repeatedly over time. Check for doneness by paying attention to what is happening in your life and how you feel about it. If you like what you're getting, keep doing it. If not, change something.

The most powerful thing about this recipe is that the ingredients are always present and being combined in equal proportions consistently over time. You are doing it right now. And you are successful at it. If you do not have a specific desire or goal you are going after, or you are unclear about it, then what you want is to stay where you are. If you are filled with doubt, you are comfortable with being timid and insecure and not trusting yourself. When you do not trust that things will work in your favor, what you can count on is that they won't. Doing nothing is in itself doing something. The ingredients continually combine, in equal proportions. You do it unconsciously, on autopilot, until you decide you want something to change. Then it gets uncomfortable because you have to examine what ill ingredient you are infusing into the recipe, and why.

You have the recipe. Mixing the four ingredients together according to the instructions creates confidence and a feeling of contentment. And when you feel good about what you are doing, you usually get favorable results. But a recipe is only as good as its ingredients. And there are correct ways and incorrect ways to combine them. So let's review each of the ingredients and how they are used.

Know What You Want

For this to be a quality ingredient it needs to be precise. This is your goal. Believing you can reach your goal, trusting all is in order and will work out, and taking action to achieve it require that you are clear on what it is you desire. *What do you really want, and why is it you want it?* These questions help identify what is truly important to you.

Knowing what you want is your goal. Knowing why you want it and declaring that it must be so is your *intention*; and both must be crystal clear. This is the vision of your future, a picture of what your life will be. Focus on the end result and how you feel about it. Whether you are aware of it or not, you always have a vision of tomorrow. It is rooted deep within your subconscious. To change it you must declare exactly what it is you desire and be passionate about it. In its purest form, your vision is the precise intention you have for your future. Impress this vision into your subconscious consistently and repeatedly.

It is important that your vision is not the omission of what you don't want. Focusing on what you would like to eliminate places the spotlight on what you don't want. This ill vision is then impressed into your subconscious. The reason many struggle with making positive changes is because they focus on what they would like to eliminate, and in so doing, more of what they want to eliminate shows up. To have a better relationship, visualize what is important to you in the ideal relationship. For health, imagine yourself living with energy and vitality, and loving yourself. More money? Imagine the income that will be accumulated, not the bills it will pay. It's normal to focus on conditions that you want to fix, but there is no fixing to be done. Nothing is broken. You just *think* it is. Instead, create what it is you prefer and experience the feeling of having it now.

The best advice I have ever been given about my vision – the things I desire and why I want them – is to write them down and review them often. Read them before going to bed at night;

read them first thing in the morning. And as you review the things you want, close your eyes and imagine how it would *feel* to have them. What you feel about your intention is the fuel that puts it into motion. Put notes up on your bathroom mirror, on your refrigerator, at your work space – wherever you can keep a constant reminder in front of you. It may feel a bit awkward. You may be shy about declaring your intention publically for others to see. Experiencing the emotion of having it as you go to sleep at night and again first thing in the morning as you set out on your day eventually eases the discomfort of sharing it with others.

I've heard it said many times that everything we do exists in one of four states. It begins as an idea. It is then written down with a plan. Action is taken on the plan. And finally it is done. Your vision – what you want and why you want it – needs a plan for action. Writing it down is the first step in this plan. It is brought forth from the ethers of your mind into physical form. From this vision you can establish intermediate goals, the things you need to do to get the job done. It is in setting these goals that your belief and trust can be challenged.

Your vision is important. It must be clear. It must be written down. And you must review it daily, experiencing the elation of making it happen. Know what you want and why you want it. When you can excavate to the core reason for doing something you want to do for those you love – something that will live long beyond you, or when the core reason is the betterment of mankind, you know that it is a worthy desire and that you will feel fulfilled when your goal is reached. There are certainly stepping stones along the way – things that are fun to have, things that are enjoyable to do with people you love to be with. Be sure to include desirable things that will propel you forward rather than superfluous luxuries. Your vision is real when you begin to meet doubt and fear with thoughts and actions that resist them. This is the discomfort that shatters most dreams. Many cower away at this point, settling back into their comfort zone to avoid the emotional burden of resisting the fear and doubt of a lofty vision. To push on, there are remaining ingredients to add to the recipe.

Believe You Can

A dream is worth pursuing when it seems *nearly* impossible; when the crystal-clear vision – the declared intent of what you want, is challenged along with your belief – the second ingredient in the recipe of life. Belief is accepting something is possible, that you deserve it, and that you can keep it once you get it. Others have done it, so why not you? It has a direct impact on your attitude about yourself and your vision. This attitude about your vision is a barometer of your belief in it. If you do not believe you deserve it, dig deeper and find out why.

What you believe yourself to be, and what you believe of the world around you, create your default way of living. They are your autopilot. The good news is that you can course-correct if you are not getting what you want. Your steering wheel is your attitude. If you are suffering from low self-esteem and prejudice toward others, pay close attention to what you watch, read, and listen to. We are inundated by negative information that has limited utility. For every piece of disparaging news there are dozens of people who are doing good deeds, making good lives for themselves, overcoming obstacles, and enjoying the wonders of life.

Your attitude about yourself and others is a key element in the ingredient of belief. Take a moment and think of those whom you highly respect for their accomplishments and ability to get things done. Consider how they accomplish tasks in a timely, calm, relaxed manner. Think of the qualities and abilities you admire in them. Which of these are skills or knowledge they have learned? Which are inherent gifts? And which are attitudes? I believe you will find that most successful people who are worthy of your respect have adopted an empowering attitude. And that attitude has everything to do with what they believe is possible.

Believe you deserve this life. Many people who give up on their vision have a self-image that denies their getting what they want. The life you live now is based on the belief you have in yourself and others. If you believe life to be unfair, that it's rigged to get you, that you can't trust others – that is what you will experience. Equally, if you believe that life is full of wonder and opportunities and that people are generally good, you will experience that.

Believe that you can keep that life once you have created it. There is no need to fall back. You can create a wonderful life and not fall victim to the hills and valleys of making gains and then losing them. You can continue to persevere, always growing, always finding bounty, and loving the lessons in all you do. The adoption of such an attitude aligns with the belief that you can do it and you deserve it.

You might believe that your life is the result of outside influences, other people, and events. You might believe that life is difficult and there is no such thing as a perfect job, a perfect relationship, perfect health, or to have it all perfectly working together. The bottom line is you are still where you are, and if you don't like it, it's up to you to do something about it. That entails believing in the vision of what you want and why you want it.

If you feel doubt, examine your belief in creating what you want and your belief in yourself. Good intentions are often doused with doubt. Having your vision clearly spelled out and visible is an essential element in believing you can get it done.

You will also be challenged by obstacles – every reason why your vision is not feasible. Your analytical mind employs every defense it can to trick you into believing your life is as good as it gets and that anything better isn't practical. When obstacles impede, trust that your vision can and will happen. Acting on a clear intention, founded with genuine belief, creates opportunity. The "how to" is not important. What is important is that you are emotionally moved by the vision you see your life to be.

Trust It Will All Work Out

There is a power that aligns circumstances with what you believe to be true. Things magically come your way based on what you think about and impress on your subconscious mind.

If you believe in a hostile universe, that is what you experience. If you believe in a loving and abundant universe, that is what you receive. It is magical, and quite mysterious. What is difficult to accept is that this powerful force is at work all the time. It is creating the conditions that support what you think about, your attitude, and your habits and activities each day.

Referring back to knowing what you want and the importance of focusing on what you desire rather than what you would like to eliminate, this magical force manifests what is on your mind. Do you want to have more patience or be more tolerant? This force will create the irritating conditions for you to be patient and tolerant. Do you want to get out of debt? This force will create the debt you wish to eliminate. Do you want to lose weight? Get ready to retain the weight you wish to eliminate, or gain more. Some have likened it to your own personal genie who says, "Your wish is my command." Unlike the popular fable, there is no limit to the wishes you can make, and each wish is granted. Often the problem is that the wish is not delivered precisely. When you wish for a new home, the genie gets to work creating the new home. But when you follow that desire with doubt that you can afford the mortgage, the genie gives you the opportunity to buy a home you cannot afford. When you wish for a new job, the genie gets busy creating it. But when you dwell on avoiding the deplorable working conditions you are currently experiencing, the genie delivers a job that has these same conditions. This power always delivers what you believe to be true. And sometimes that belief is buried deep in your subconscious mind.

Accepting this third ingredient – trust it will all work out – can be summarized as faith. This is not necessarily in the context of religion, though it certainly can be. There is a force at our disposal that is creative and without limits, whether you care to consider it magical, or divine, or not. Simply trust that mysterious coincidences can happen, and they will. This mystery can only be experienced. Words do it little justice. Accept that the conditions, people, and circumstances that show up in your life are the wishes being granted by your genie – the thoughts and beliefs you have about your life and the world around you.

A good way to fit this ingredient into the recipe is to call on your intuition – your gut feeling. Faith is trusting your intuition to guide you. And guide you it will, with a clear vision of what it is you want to achieve. Faith is also trusting that you do not need to know the answers – you do not need to know how you are going to succeed. You trust that the resources you need – the people, the education, the money, and the time – will become available when needed. When you have a vision, and you are looking into the Uncomfortable Zone wondering how you are going to accomplish it and fighting disbelief and fear, have faith that the answers will appear when you let them.

This is a power that is greater than you. When you feel anxious, stressed, and out of harmony deep inside, it is this power that is calling and challenging your old beliefs. Your intuition is a message from within. If you get unfavorable results from trusting it, a couple of things could be happening: Either there is an ingredient in the recipe that is missing or compromised, or this apparent failure could simply be the door opening to another opportunity, the details of which are obscure at this time.

When declaring what it is you truly want, and believing it is possible, you don't need to know how it's going to happen. As soon as you let go of how it's going to look and how you are going to accomplish it, the magic begins. It is in this ingredient – trust that it will all work out – that the "how to" appears. All you have to do is be very clear about what it is you desire, and why – your vision; believe it can happen; and take some meaningful steps in that direction: do something.

Do Something

Solutions magically appear when you take repetitive action on what you believe you deserve and can have. Taking action on a goal, with clear intent and a firm belief that it will be accomplished, creates the conditions and circumstances that support accomplishing it. Have a crystal-clear vision – know what you want and why you want it. Believe you can have it and deserve it. And once you trust everything will somehow work out in a magical and mysterious way, taking action on what you want is invigorating. The magical genie is expecting you to take action. The more you act on your ideas and inspiration, the more you get in return. You will feel as though you are on top of the world.

Action, in alignment with your belief, is invigorating. Action that opposes your belief is drudgery. Action toward a precise goal – one that is specific, measurable, achievable, and with a specific time line – is empowering. Without a clear goal, action is nothing more than hope.

Taking action toward getting something you want, believing you can have it, and trusting it will all work in your favor can be invigorating, yet intimidating. Clarity about your purpose creates an attitude of success, yet it is fragile. Momentum is easily lost when your default way of thinking does everything it can to keep you from doing something you have not done before. This is when it becomes uncomfortable to do the things you don't want to do, knowing you must.

When I looked back on all of my study and why I wasn't getting the results I wanted, I wondered what I was doing wrong. Instead of looking into why the recipe wasn't working, I was seeking the ever-elusive missing piece. In other words, the action I was taking was to continually seek the solution to why I was failing. This led to failure every time, because my focus was on something missing.

The irony is nothing was missing. The recipe was producing the precise results to be expected from the ingredients I was using. I consciously wanted a strong, nurturing relationship. I wanted financial liberty. I wanted a vibrant, healthy body. The underlying intention was that something was wrong with me and I needed to fix it before I could have those things. Every recipe has a name, and the name of the recipe I had successfully mastered is *self-sabotage*.

When you do not trust this process, the results are unpredictable, as I found out. I felt that I was broken and needed to search further for some secret tip to fix me. I was injecting doubt instead of trust, and sabotaging my efforts. The recipe works. Every time. But when an ingredient is compromised, the recipe changes and your result becomes more of the condition you already have. What you have in your life now, whether you like it or not, you conjured up in your own kitchen; it is the recipe that works for you. And it has worked flawlessly and will continue to do so until you change.

The steps you take to change your life must be significant and have purpose. They become significant when they come into alignment with your belief and trust that you can and will do it. They have purpose when you are steadfast in what you desire. The recipe is precise and flawless. If you are using ingredients for a prosperous, joyful life, you'll be successful at creating it. If you are using ingredients for being stuck, frustrated, and despondent, you'll be successful at creating that.

This pretty much sums up the recipe of life. All four ingredients combined in equal portions consistently over time produce results. And if you recall from the prior chapter, there is a nice safety net in this formula: *pay attention to what is happening and how you feel about it*. If you are not getting the results you want, change something. Take a look at the results you are creating and understand what need is being fulfilled. The emotion you feel about the results you are creating will lead you to decide whether or not the underlying need is still important. If not, let it go. If it is, seek out a different way to satisfy this need *and* create a different result.

Either way you will challenge your pattern of predictable and tolerable habits. It will be uncomfortable. It is supposed to be. Having your cake and eating it too means that you sometimes take a bite of the cake baked with the lasagna recipe. You need this taste test to know what to adjust in your life.

Know Your Fear, Know Your Truth

Success is the ability to go from one failure to another with no loss of enthusiasm.
– Anonymous

"**N**o fear" is the biggest, most profound lie on the planet. Everyone has fear. If you were to chain someone who claims to have no fear in a cage with a hungry carnivore, they might change their story. Of course this is an extreme and unlikely example. There are things that rouse fear in each of us. This fear is real, and it is the reaction we have to experiencing something we deem a threat to our safety.

Risk is the choice to gain something while accepting there is a chance of failure. Our emotional feelings about the potential failure play out as fear. *What if I lose my money if I do this? What if I remain broke if I do not? What will others think? Will they be offended?* All the questions that come up when taking a risk beg for answers. Lacking answers, we experience fear. The more risk, the more fear.

When the pursuit of your dream is met with fear, the Uncomfortable Zone is created. It is at this point many turn back, unwilling to make a change and go after what it is they really want in life. Their life story has them in a repeating cycle, playing it safe, doing the same thing day after day, each day looking much the same as the one before – all with a glimmer of hope that someday something will happen to set them free of this imprisoning cycle. The days move into months, the months into years, and all there is to hold on to is regret, simply because they were not willing to do something different, to be uncomfortable for a short period of time and break the cycle.

Most of us go on day after day following the same recipe, doing the same things, and little changes. We do have an inherent desire to grow and flourish. It is stronger in some of us than in others. When that fire is stoked to make a change, there is the realization that you are in a rut; life is becoming mundane, with less purpose. To get out of your rut, know your fear. Know your truth. Assess why you fear making a change, because if there were little or no fear, you would probably already be doing it. It is that fear that acts as a governor, keeping you in your safe cycle of thinking, being, and doing, all the while producing predictable results.

Know fear. Know *your* fear. Know it well. It comes cleverly disguised. If personified, your fear is the CEO of a large organization with managers who have one simple responsibility:

to keep you from making a change. It is *your* fear. It is totally unique to you. You created it. It is shared with no one. And only you can confront it. To do so – to have an interview with that CEO, you must first know them.

The first thing to understand about fear is that it is a part of you. Fear is your anticipated emotional response to events that have already occurred. It is based on what you think you know and founded on the emotional pain you experienced in the past. F.E.A.R. is popularly expressed as an acronym for False Evidence Appearing Real, the concept being that fear is based on the perception of events having an unfavorable outcome. However, fear is real. It is not false. The evidence, too, is real, at least as the facts go. It is the interpretation of the facts that makes the evidence appear threatening.

The next thing to understand about fear is that it does what it is perfectly designed to do: keep you safe. Fear is not a bad thing. You just need to remember that it is extremely effective at keeping you from making the choices you consciously want to make. It is only when it prevents you from taking a harmless action that it becomes a problem. F.E.A.R. also stands for Forget Everything And Return, which is what most people do when they are afraid – they return to what is safe and predictable.

Accept that you are afraid, and in so doing give yourself permission to experience the fear and explore deeper to its source. Understand why it is you are afraid. Go ahead and assess the worst possible things that could happen. Jot them down in a list. Take a look at that list and ask yourself why each is unacceptable. Delve deeply as to why you have an emotional response to taking that risk. Don't judge yourself. Look back into your life story for events that stirred this emotion. Explore those events and the meaning you placed on them. The fear you face is a calling from your soul that you can choose. This calling is challenged by an autonomous belief that is in place to keep you safe based on the way you perceive your past.

For each item on your worst-case-scenario list, discard those that are truly improbable, and for the rest consider what precautions can you take to avoid them. In other words, do not ignore the danger, but simply step forward in a responsible way. There is no reason to make an irresponsible choice that would add another negative experience to your life story. The focus is on making an *informed* decision and moving forward with confidence and certainty.

When you explore the list of things you fear could go wrong, ask yourself why you are focusing on the risk rather than the gain. A more fruitful exercise is to ask yourself, "What if…?" followed by the positive outcome. What if I get the job? What if the new business is fulfilling and prosperous? What if this person is perfect for me? Feel the emotion of it actually happening. Truly embrace the joy of your dream coming true.

To summarize these steps, do the following to find the courage to step into your own fear and pursue what it is you desire:

- Accept you are afraid, with no judgment, giving yourself permission to be so.
- Explore why it is you are afraid. Make a list of the worst-case scenarios that could happen.

- For each scenario:
  - Ask why it is so bad. What is in your life story that is stirring up such emotion?
  - What is the likelihood of the "bad" thing happening? And what can you do to ease your mind? What precautions can you take to make it less risky?
  - Then ask, "What if...?" followed by one or more positive outcomes, and how they would feel.

The objective of this exercise is to examine what it is you fear and why it is holding you back from making a change in your life. You have plenty of evidence to support your fear. As long as you believe the evidence to be true, you will hesitate to take meaningful action. In asking why it is you are afraid, you might remember times when someone did you wrong. By looking at those times when you were hurt you will find the roots of your fear. Accept that those painful times did happen, and that the emotion you felt *at that time* was appropriate. It is no longer necessary to feel that pain in the life you are now living. It might not have been fair. Someone did something wrong and it hurt. The event took place in the past. It is just your ever-efficient mind and body doing what they can to avoid your ever getting hurt again that get in your way. The fear you have from past trauma is creating what you believe to be true today.

As important as understanding fear is knowing your truth. The basis of your truth is what you believe about yourself and others. Your truth dictates the choices you make and the actions you take. Your emotional reaction to an event supports how you view yourself and the world in which you live. Your belief is reinforced and verified to be true. And you continue to live by this truth until it is challenged by a life event that makes you question it, or you simply decide it's time for a change.

Your truth is not based solely on facts; it is your emotional interpretation of the facts surrounding events you experienced in the past. Because we each have our own life experiences, our truth is unique to us. The same event can result in different truths for different people based on their interpretation of it. This is much in line with following your life map. As events happen, the meaning you place on those events usually follows your favorite routes. You continue to go about your life being cautious of others, procrastinating, avoiding risk, and being a victim to events that took place long ago. Unless there is a conscious effort to take a new route, the meaning of those events is what you believe to be your truth. The fear you have of the past is the foundation of the truth you live by today.

The above exercise – to allow yourself to be afraid and explore why it is you are scared – also allows you to identify why you avoid doing what is needed to make a change. When you embrace the emotion you experience at the wall, unable to step forward and not wanting to turn back, you can identify your fear and the truth by which you live. There is a change you want to make in your life. What are you feeling? Why are you feeling that way? What are the stories you have made up about your life that are the bricks and mortar in the wall holding you back? Reflecting on these questions is the key to challenging your truth and overcoming the fear that keeps you from living the dreams you desire.

One way to challenge your truth is to reconsider situations in which your emotions were triggered in the past. How could they have been interpreted in a different way? Practice challenging your emotional reactions by applying that different interpretation to simple triggers that occur in your daily life, and it will happen more quickly and naturally when a critical triggering event occurs.

If you recall, there are three defenses when making a change: emotional, mental, and metaphysical. They are evidence that your mind and body are working in perfect harmony. It is your emotion that triggers the reaction. Your mental defense provides the opportunity to react in a different way; you have the power to choose how you react to an event. Quelling the emotion by choosing to react in a different way is eventually recorded in your neural network as a new program that can be called on when similar events occur. This process of reprogramming your brain takes work because the metaphysical force that is ever-present to create resistance pushes you back. With persistence and determination you can learn to respond rather than react.

Fear of doing something new is the result of your body and mind working in perfect harmony to protect you and keep you out of danger's way. Explore it. Understand what you fear and why. Until you come to understand the source of your fear and that it is in place to keep you safe, you will continue to avoid taking action on things that seem uncomfortable.

Know your truth as well. What you believe to be true presents itself in every event you experience. Holding steadfast to that truth accumulates evidence about whether or not you are capable of making a change. If you believe others to be benevolent, caring, trustworthy, and kind, you will experience events to support that truth. If you believe others to be greedy, narcissistic, and mean, you will experience just that.

What you believe to be true will eventually manifest into the conditions and people in your life that support that truth. Fear will do everything it can to prevent you from changing that picture. Know what it is you believe to be true and why. Know what you fear and how it stops you from getting what you want. Your fear creates your truth.

Pay Off the Debt on Your Life

Instead of trying to make yourself perfect, give yourself the freedom to make it an adventure, and go ever upward.
– Drew Houston

Most of us incur debt to buy the things we have in life. We owe money to a bank for our stuff. The desire to immediately have the stuff was important enough to sign a promissory note. After a few payments we still love the stuff, yet not the payments. So we do what we can to pay off the debt as quickly as possible.

There is a similar debt to be paid on life. There are things we want from others, and a price paid to get them – not payable to a bank, friend, or family member. The payment cannot be measured, yet it comes at a very high interest rate. The longer you defer paying this debt, the larger it grows. This debt is the discomfort it takes to make a change in your life and take unencumbered ownership of it so that you are not under a lien or the expectation of others – a life that is not constrained by fearing what could happen based on the emotional impacts of events in the past.

Settling for less than you deserve is the greatest debt your soul can endure. Years ago when I was in college, I struggled with a choice: to pursue a path to composing music or to be an accountant. Music has been my passion to this day. There are melodies and rhythms always dancing in the ballroom of my mind. An equal passion is the dynamics of business. I revel in the thoughts that are turned into goods and services, then brought to market; and in how people receive these products through their choices to buy.

I had a choice to make. Which was going to be my major? I chose a business degree with emphasis in accounting, and not regretfully so. This career path served me quite well. Understanding how to compile a set of company financial statements carried me far. I often think, though, that the decision to pursue business was fueled by my need for my parents' approval, especially my father's. I did feel a bit obligated because they were financing the bulk of my education. But I furthered this choice by actually doing both. I pursued the career of an accountant and was a part-time musician. It was quite fulfilling in that the career in business provided an ample income and the music was a wonderful artistic outlet.

But not everyone has the opportunity to avoid the regret that I was able to avoid. There are a set of victim roles we play to justify the debt of regret in our lives. We each play at least one of these. And sometimes we play one role at work, another at home, and perhaps even another in social settings. In so doing, there are needs we want satisfied that are neglected. Over time the neglect adds up as a debt we have on a piece of our life.

- The need to be right
- The need to be not wrong
- The need to belong
- The need to be recognized

The need to be right is founded on the belief that there are rules we must follow as members of a society. There is right, there is wrong. And each has its consequences. The need to be right leads to defining rules of conduct for a group and the individuals who make up that group. It goes further to taking a stand on defining the rules and seeing that they are enforced. There is a right way, and anything less is unacceptable. In intimate, committed relationships in which fidelity is one of those rules, cheating is not acceptable. Even the fantasy of doing so is not acceptable. The victimization of the need to be right is when we get so invested in making sure the rules are followed that compassion for others is neglected. The debt being accumulated on the need to be right is that others may see you lacking compassion and being stubborn, inflexible, and obsessed with the black-and-white of things. You are more interested in getting results than in connecting with others.

The need to be not wrong sounds synonymous with the need to be right, yet there is a difference. There is a humorous story of an executive in a hot air balloon, lost in the fog. She finds an engineer on the ground and asks where she is. The engineer replies that she is approximately twenty feet off the ground in the basket of a balloon. The frustrated executive replies that she must be talking with an engineer because he responded quite accurately with information that is useless in her predicament. The engineer replies that he must be talking with an executive who is lost because she doesn't know where she's going or how to get there, yet for some reason it is his fault. The executive is operating from the need to be right, following the rules. The engineer has the need to be not wrong, providing a precise response to the question asked. The debt to be paid on the need to be not wrong is in missing the spontaneous joy of life. In this debt, the beauty and mystery of living is obscured by to-do lists and making sure everything goes as planned. Responses are logical, to the point, carefully calculated, and very accurate. Relationships can be compromised in the need to be not wrong as others deem you overly pragmatic. Joy is lost in the analysis of every detail. It is concentrating on one tree and missing the beauty of the forest.

The need to belong is the need for love, compassion, and servitude. Though this personality can be extremely loyal, sometimes it is to the extreme of a fault. They live to serve others. The debt to be paid on the need to belong is in giving everyone and everything else priority over oneself. Actions and choices are focused on making others comfortable and happy, often at the expense of being comfortable and happy themselves. They tend to take direction well, except from themselves.

The need to be recognized is the desire to be in the limelight, the life of the party, the one everyone wants to be around. The debt to be paid on the need to be recognized is in failing to keep agreements and not doing what you say you will do when you say you will do it. Over time you earn the reputation of not following through. You are often dismayed by the number of projects you have started and not completed.

To further describe these four victim roles, let's use having a cup of coffee as an example. Those who have a need to be right expect their coffee to be a certain temperature, served in the correct style of cup, with the appropriate condiments and utensils readily available to satisfy any preference. Those who have a need to be not wrong ensure that the precise amount of water and coffee are used, following a defined recipe, and provide the correct cup and utensils that are of the best value. Those who have a need to belong care most about enjoying the coffee with others, in conversation and emotional connection. Those with a need to be recognized care only that they get the damned coffee!: "C'mon, let's get this day going… there are things to do, people to see!"

Any one of us can fall into any of these victim roles. And we are not limited to just one. For years I moved back and forth between the need to be recognized and the need to be not wrong. I enjoyed life just enough to get by while doing what was expected of me and making sure I had documented proof that I was living up to the expectations of others – or more accurately, living up to my belief of what was expected of me. For that I expected recognition and accolades. When I did not feel appreciated, I dug deeper into doing what I thought I was supposed to be doing and making sure I had evidence that I was doing nothing wrong. Focusing on doing what I thought was expected, and yearning for the reward of attention and acknowledgment, I lost sight of what was important to me. I was living up to the expectations of others over my own. And I was craving a response from others rather than being satisfied with who I was and the paths I had chosen.

I recommend looking into yourself to see what needs you want fulfilled and why. Which of the needs are you: the need to be right, to be not wrong, to belong, or to be recognized? Ask yourself why you have this need. It has developed over many years, starting in your youth. Operating from this state, embrace what it is you have to offer. Knowing your strength can help you overcome your weakness. For the need to be right, be righteous about being of service to others, connecting, and having compassion. For the need to be not wrong, allow yourself to be relaxed, spontaneous, and fun-loving. For the need to belong, have compassion for yourself. Learn to say yes to yourself. For the need to be recognized, step into the spotlight of being dependable and detail-oriented.

Paying off the debt in your life entails recognizing and empowering your strengths to overcome your weaknesses. Doing so may seem like a nuisance, a chore, or perhaps frightening, yet remaining in debt creates *passive stress*, when the desire to have something better battles against all the justifications for why it is not possible. You know there are things you need to be doing differently; you are just not doing them. You lose sleep at night worrying about what you need to change. There is an underlying current of remorse that gnaws at you, not leaving you alone. This is a desire that beckons you to make a change.

Surrender or Give Up

For after all, the best thing one can do when it is raining is let it rain.
– Henry Wadsworth Longfellow

I looked at the ring on my left hand, not believing what I saw. One of the diamonds was missing out of my wedding band. My wife had given it to me on our wedding day. Three diamonds of equal size, set into a simple yet beautiful band of white gold. Each represented the love that blesses my life. Understanding our family love, her choice was well-considered and deliberate: three stones for my love for each of my three children; three for my love for each of my brothers; and three for the love between me, my mother, and my father. Simultaneously these three gems encompassed the enduring love and support in my life. She had it custom made with these loves in mind. But the love she most wanted to convey with these three stones was one to represent me, one to represent her, and the other to represent the love that bound us.

Now one was gone. And I had to accept that my search for it was near hopeless. The loss took place at a business event I was attending with dozens of people moving about from room to room. I first looked around my chair, then checked my pockets, and gazed through the room. I excused myself and began to retrace my steps, eyes locked on the greyish carpet, hoping for a ray of light to glisten from this tiny gem. There was none.

I could have given up and just waited to see how everything was to play out. I could have given up by staying quiet, depressed, and down about my bad luck. My mind would have been preoccupied with thoughts of contacting the jeweler, haggling about the poor quality of the setting, how much it would cost, the time it would take, and what to tell my wife.

Instead of giving up, I surrendered. I accepted the situation for what it was. This wasn't the first time a gem had been lost from a piece of jewelry. It was not a profound sign of ill omens to come. It wasn't a huge financial setback creating a hardship in our lives. The loss had no significance in my life except what I chose to place on it. The diamond could be replaced. And even though a replacement could never be the original, what it represented was steadfast, irreplaceable, and invaluable. The ring, with or without the diamond, was a daily reminder that I had the support of this love all around me. By surrendering, the emotion dissolved and no longer gripped my thoughts.

It was at that point that I felt relief. The search was over because it seemed pointless to look for a small diamond in light grey carpet. There was a lot of area to cover. And I didn't remember exactly where I had walked. I wasn't sure when I had last looked closely at the ring. Perhaps the stone had dislodged prior to even entering the building. Many people had been scurrying around. If it was there, it had probably been trampled into the carpet, destined to be an audible pop as it was sucked up in the night crew's vacuum. And that was now okay.

The choice to surrender is an uncomfortable one. It challenges all that is known to be true. By surrendering, I gave up being concerned about what my wife would think. That was her business, not mine. My thoughts battled about whether I should be concerned. If I truly loved her then I must worry now and do everything I could to make it right. I fought thoughts that warned me of her disappointment, which would certainly ensue. The cost, the inconvenience, the faulty workmanship of the jeweler were all floating about in my head, demanding my attention. I made a conscious effort to keep them at bay. I accepted the situation for what it was, devoid of emotion. The diamond was lost. And now I somehow felt as though all would fall into order in getting it replaced.

I could have given up and wallowed in angry misery. This is a state I understand well, and it is so easy for me to do. I have been there many times in my life, and often see others in this state. It requires little effort to create a hopeless, optionless world where something or someone is always to blame. It takes no responsibility. It requires no thought. When life sucks, it doesn't feel good. Blaming someone or something else is an easy way to dispel bad feelings.

Surrendering to the situation is a disciplined effort. It can be difficult. It takes a conscious effort to step out of the drama and move beyond old stories from past events and the stigma of what others will think. When life sucks, surrendering is taking responsibility for the choices that led to the sucky life. Surrendering is accepting the moment for what it is – a moment; nothing more. When emotion is high, your ability to think is low. Surrendering lightens emotion and gives weight to rational thought:

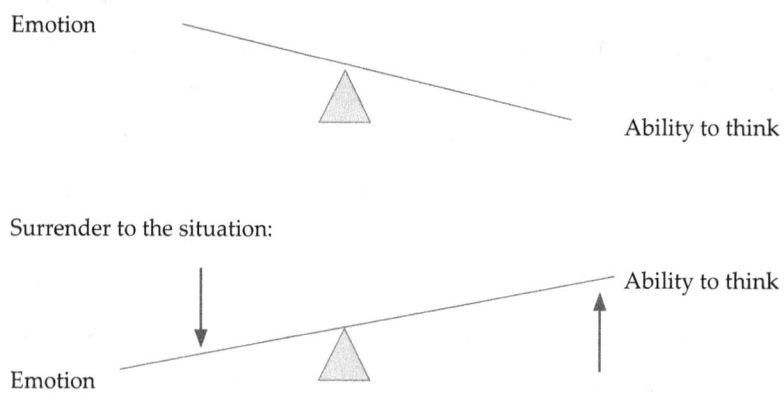

What I chose to do next regarding my ring was an interesting lesson. I approached one of the commentators at the business event and asked him to make an announcement. Quite frankly I wasn't very hopeful, but I did have faith that if someone had found the diamond they would be happy to return it. The commentator's response caught me by surprise. I first thought it

SURRENDER OR GIVE UP

was an inappropriate joke. He pointed to the floor and candidly asked, "Do you mean like that one?" I cautioned him not to jest with me, as I did not want to stir up the emotions that had battled to take command of my actions and words. He bent down, picked up something from the floor where we were standing, and handed it to me. Yes, it was the missing diamond!

To surrender is not to give up. Giving up is entering a state of complacency, at the mercy of the world around you. It reinforces what you believe of the world and allows you to be a victim of this belief. Giving up is abandoning free will and wallowing in the emotions of failure and loss. When emotion is high, the ability to see options and make rational decisions is very low. Emotions are your body's way of confirming what you believe to be true. As long as you remain a victim of your emotions, this belief becomes your truth.

To surrender is to accept what is and let go of the emotional baggage associated with it. Rather than being victimized by a hopeless situation, become a part of it. Accept your responsibility of choice. You did things and said stuff that got you where you are. When you surrender and release your emotions about the situation, you are free to make a rational choice rather than an emotional one.

To surrender is to go with the flow. When faced with a life event that is challenging, it's up to you to decide whether you are defeated or it is simply a turning point in a scheme that is beyond your knowing and is for the good. To surrender is to accept that what is, is simply what is. You can interpret any emotion you experience as a defense and as retreating to an imaginary place of safety. Experience that emotion to its fulfilment as quickly as possible, get over it, and just accept what has happened.

Giving up is a despondent acceptance that there is no hope. It is continuing to play out your life story following the script from past events. It is to fall victim to the uncertainties of life and how unpredictable it can be. It supports the belief that the world is hostile and that you must always be aware of danger. Focusing on the danger drives choices and actions that place danger in your path, providing more opportunities to give up.

Imagine how many movie scripts would have to be changed if we all understood that by surrendering we are simply accepting conditions as they are. Imagine that demanding that a foe surrender really meant "Stop this silly fight, come be our prisoner so you can get your head straight, then escape and take up the fight again." Though it wouldn't work in a movie script, that is what needs to be done in a situation that seems hopeless. Surrender. Give up the silly fight. Stop resisting what is and accept it as a new and unique challenge. It could be an opportunity in disguise. With emotion creating a sense of despair that all is lost, any chance for another option – a new opportunity – is lost as well.

Surrendering is accepting what is, releasing the emotion, dusting yourself off, and getting back up and going at it again. I often wonder what discoveries lie in our untapped minds – what cures for illness, advances in technology, peace between warring nations, or knowledge to be shared would come forth if just a few good people had not given up. And how many of these opportunities are now buried in the minds of those who have passed.

When faced with a situation that appears hopeless, instead of throwing your hands in the air and giving up, surrender to the event. It will clear your mind and let you think freely and creatively. When you expel the emotions of defeat you might find that a solution is just around the corner.

You Are Okay

*Today you are you! That is truer than true!
There is no one alive who is you-er than you!*
— Dr. Seuss

There is an important thing you need to know about yourself: You are not broken. You are not dealing with some flaw that you must overcome. You are not less than others. There is nothing that needs to be fixed. If you feel downtrodden, inferior, unworthy, inadequate, or flawed in any way, you are not. That is only how you *feel*. It is an emotional state. It is only temporary. However, the more you remain feeling inadequate, the more comfortable you will be there.

Activity with an infusion of emotion creates a habit. Once you begin enjoying the benefits of being down and defeated, you tend to remain there. Your emotional response to things that happen is a complex process of chemicals produced by and released into your body. When threatened you react by protecting yourself. And the more you experience emotion as a part of life, the more you want to experience events that stir emotion. It is as though you form an addiction to the emotional response. This is true even for self-deprecating emotions such as anxiety, depression, jealousy, and unworthiness. Once an emotion becomes engrained in your personality, you make choices that support your having that emotion. You get your fix. You can be addicted to winning, or losing. You can be addicted to happiness, or despair.

There are benefits to any emotional state. Obviously there are benefits of being positive, upbeat, happy, and productive. These folks are fun to be around. The benefits are being connected with others and creating fulfilling lives. But what could possibly be the benefits of being down, neglected, sickly, or despondent? For those who are miserable, there is sympathy, compassion, charity, and acknowledgment of being a victim of the evils of the world. When seeking sympathy from others, they receive compassion and charity – for a while. Then those giving it run dry at some point. They no longer invite the glum person to social events. They become the victim's assailants of life's misery.

I have observed that like-minded people associate with each other. I struggle not to use the "birds of a feather flock together" cliché, yet that's what I am talking about. Another is "Misery loves company." A person who complains about their life always has sympathizers. They, too, are complaining about their lives. Now throw in someone who challenges their complaints, suggesting that their misery is merely a choice and that they have everything they need to make a change and create the lives they desire. Even if they do so with love and good intent, such a challenger would not be well received. Most likely they would be judged as insensitive, cold, and righteous.

We do not have to look very far to find something to complain about or someone who shares the same complaint. This is an aspect of human psychology that fascinates me and is just as perplexing. It seems to be easier to complain than it is to compliment. I cannot help but think that it is in pride that this prevails. To find criticism in others serves no purpose other than to elate the ego: "They did a despicable thing. I would never do that. Therefore I am good and they are not." Though this thinking is fallacious, many do it. I believe this is why there is so much negative media bombarding us, and why a movie or book must have a villain; it seems to fill this need. It provides a sense of character, feedback if you will, that satisfies our self-worth. And when a need such as this is filled, it sells.

Receiving feedback that there are many in this world who need to be held accountable for their actions eliminates the need to be accountable for our own actions and the outcomes they produce. It supports thinking, "I might say and do things that do minor harm to others, but I am not as bad as most. And I can live with that." Yet I feel most people are good. They care about others and they are loving, courteous, and want to be a positive influence on others. They generally have a gentle demeanor and a good attitude. They just have some personality traits that yearn for attention. When they are not getting the attention they desire, they choose to create the life circumstances they need to get their fix.

When it comes to making a change in their lives – a permanent transformation that is just outside their realm of belief – many confront that change with excuses such as limited money, not enough time, being away from the family, work obligations, yard work, paying the bills, or emptying the dishwasher. Because the change is just outside their level of belief, they sabotage all efforts to make it happen. Outwardly they are upbeat and positive, with a "can do" attitude. Yet deep down they hurt. They believe it is possible to have the life they desire, with vibrant health and deep, meaningful relationships, but they just don't believe *they* can have it *now*. Someday perhaps, but not now. For others perhaps, but not them.

They have convinced themselves that it is their calling to have less – less money, less recognition; or to be in ill health; or to be lonely; or to have meaningless lives. I have certainly experienced this myself. There were times I felt that I just didn't have what it took to have the life I dreamed of; to live where I wanted to; to have the deep, meaningful relationship I yearned for; to be in wonderful health, living life and loving it. I felt that it was not worth striving for more, that I was inadequate and not worthy of such dreams. The feeling of being inadequate is a perfect justification for avoiding the anxiety that comes when dreams do not seem possible. Rather than make an effort, it is much easier to withdraw into the ease of simply accepting less.

The feeling of being flawed comes when making comparisons to others. If there were no scale on which to compare worth and accomplishments, the only thing driving desire would be dreams and necessity. Let me explain. For a moment, remove from your mind the comparisons you make between your accomplishments and others'. Forget about the romantic relationships others have. Forget about their jobs, the homes they live in, the vacations they take. Forget about their contributions to society and their recognition. Forget about their skills, their bodies, and their ages. Without all those external comparisons in the way, assess what it is you want, and why. Let's say you dream of having a new home. Is it to have more space for the family? This desire is rooted in providing comfort for your family. If the intent is to move to a safer neighborhood, that is a desire to provide safety; it's more of a necessity. Now compare the desire to provide a new home for the sake of your family with desiring a new home in order to keep up with others, feeling slighted because you don't have the same success they have. You do not know your neighbor's motivation for living in their home. They may not like living there and perhaps may envy the home in which you live.

If you think you are anything less than perfect, I would have to ask, "Compared to what?" And in making that comparison, really consider whether or not it is a realistic one. Are you comparing yourself to an image you have constructed in your mind of someone else's life? You are perfectly capable of experiencing what you need to experience to have an enjoyable life. In being perfect you have the ability to change, and whether you change for better or worse is your choice. Changing does not mean you are less than perfect now; this is your current state, and it is different from where you were years ago and where you can be years hence. When you continue to strive for what you want, whether you get it or not you will change. It comes down to choice and perspective. If you find yourself feeling inadequate and unworthy of having more, you will feel the passive stress of remaining complacent as your dreams go by. If you instead choose to do something about it, set a plan, follow it, assess your progress, and adjust, you will feel empowered and enjoy a sense of having accomplished something.

If you are feeling inadequate, look at the comparisons you are making. It is quite normal to compare yourself to family members, friends, coworkers, or those in a social group you belong to. You might compare yourself to those in the media, and feel like you are not living up to how you should feel, what you should be doing, or with whom you should be doing it. This comparison is deceptive because you usually do not know their entire life story and whether or not they are living a fulfilled life.

Perhaps you have some emotional scars from the bumps and bruises of life, or traumatic things have happened to you, either physical or emotional. This does not make you a flawed person. Even if you have lost limbs, suffer from disease, or have had a debilitating condition since birth, there is nothing wrong with you. You may be injured, but you are not broken. You can repair much of the damage that has occurred in your life. There are countless examples of people who have risen above their current conditions and created meaningful lives. You can too. Because you have it in you. We all do.

When you examine how others have overcome obstacles or challenges like yours, be sure to make a fair comparison. Avoid the mindset of "Maybe they could do it, but not I." Let it be an inspiration to see others who have persevered and fought for what they wanted.

Granted, some people have psychological ailments or mental illnesses that need professional medical attention. I can certainly respect that. Our minds are powerful and fertile, yet delicate. Once something goes seriously wrong it does take the qualified and experienced help of others to get back on track. And some have suffered physical damage to their brains such as head injuries and strokes. For these there is professional help available and continuing advances in medical technology. Yet recovery is dependent on the attitude one holds for themselves and the desire to enjoy life.

When I struggled, I questioned myself many times. Was there something wrong with my brain? Did I have some kind of psychological dysfunction that foiled any effort to make a difference in my life? Or was it just the way I was born and raised – something from my past that I could not change? It certainly seemed to me something was broken. And to fix it, I dove deep into personal development. Not much changed. Each year I found I was living the same life, repeating the same choices. Many others were able to rise above their circumstances and make changes in their lives, but because I could not, something was obviously wrong. The best way I could reconcile the feelings of being damaged or unworthy was to retreat and simply settle for less.

Yet now I am generally at peace. There are still those times when I fall into my old ways. There are times I feel lost, lack confidence, or feel unmotivated or victimized. It has been through accepting these feelings as normal that I know I am in perfect functioning order. If I am feeling down, that acceptance allows me to lift myself up again. I enjoy my life and am excited about the wonderful things that are happening. I look forward to each new day, new people to meet, new things to do, new ideas to explore. I feel fulfilled and confident. Events continue to occur that further fuel and fulfill me. And it only took a minor course correction to create this. I just had to make a conscious effort to change the way I think about things and question the choices I make, and if I do not get the results I desire, make a course correction. I am not broken, and I never was. In fact, everything in my body was in perfect working order.

I believe you can experience this kind of transformation too. If you find yourself making the same old choices and remaining stymied in your unchanging life, you are not inferior, uneducated, or sick. You have most likely convinced yourself that it is okay, for now, to be where you are and who you are. You have made it okay to settle for less by believing you are not capable of having more. This is normal. There is nothing broken in being satisfied with your life as it is. There is nothing wrong with being at ease, comfortable with things as they are. The point at which it becomes an issue is when you truly desire something but justify not having it due to being inadequate in some way. This creates passive stress, when the desire to have something better battles against all the justifications for why it is not possible. You are planting the seed of thought that you are not capable, yet deep inside you know you are able, willing, and deserving of what it is you want. Maybe a new career excites you, yet you justify not pursuing it because you don't think you can find the time and money to attend the required training or you don't think you are smart enough to enroll in the training. Perhaps you desire a better relationship but believe the perfect partner does not exist. Or you want to volunteer in your community and cannot find the time. When there is something you want battling against the reasons why you are denied having it, passive stress is created.

    It is a matter of finding inspiration rather than settling for discouragement. It is a matter of adopting a new perspective. When I get discouraged and feel inadequate, I take a look at the many who have created wonderful lives. I make sure I read about those I have not met and associate with those I can to see what I can learn from the way they think. If I catch myself making a comparison between someone's wonderful life and mine, I ask myself, "Do I really know that much about their whole life?" And the answer is always "*No. I am making up a story about them.*" By forming a fictitious vision in my mind of who they are, what they do, and how they do it, and believing they are truly happy in the way I would want to be, I create stress for myself. If I do not sever those thoughts, they will fester into a belief that I am less than adequate, or unworthy, and I'll feel miserable about it. Unless I make a conscious decision to make a change, I will retreat to one of my old comfort zones where I conform, become complacent, and settle for less, with the intention of feeling safe.

If instead I see that I can make a difference in my life – that it will involve taking chances, behaving in a new way, challenging my thoughts, and assessing the results that stem from my actions – I experience the exciting tension of the unknown rather than the stress of passivity. This is stepping up to the zone and facing your fears head-on. When you make the choice to have a better life, and you are not willing to tolerate a lesser life any longer, take action. Know the emotional reasons why you want it. Be passionate. And when you run into obstacles and setbacks, it is not because you did something wrong; it is because you are learning. There is no need to feel that a defeat is due to any ineptitude on your part.

When life is frustrating and the struggle to keep up is an uphill battle, remember that all is actually in order, working as it should. It might seem as though life is not fair. But even with all the planning and steps you take to avoid making a mistake, sometimes mistakes are made. It might seem that others have abandoned you or that they do not care. But in growth there is a period of struggle and challenge. Your mind is doing all it can to make you retreat to where it once was. Even if you are miserable in your comfort zone, your mind knows you can survive there. It is not a threat to be miserable.

Do not be surprised or discouraged by setbacks. They do not mean you are inadequate; they mean you are learning to think in a different way. You are learning a new way to channel your beliefs into the thoughts that drive the choices and actions you make. Mistakes and upsets are part of that experience. All of the conditions in your life – who you are, how you react, what you feel – are evidence that you are in perfect working order. Just remember that you have the power to choose differently at any time. Doing so is uncomfortable, and that is normal as well.

We each have our challenges. Things might not go as planned. Your life might be in total chaos. You might suffer financial hardships or poor health, or yearn for that perfect relationship. Your dreams being out of reach does not mean you are broken or flawed in any way. In fact, it is evidence you are perfect in your creation. Your mind serves many purposes, one of which is to keep you safe. When you venture out into making a change, you must rewire your subconscious mind to accept a new way of thinking. It is uncomfortable because it is supposed to be. Even though it is uncomfortable, that does not mean you have to suffer.

Hold On Tight

The best thing to hold onto in life is each other.
– Audrey Hepburn

When my granddaughter was two years old, she loved to swing on a swing. A beaming grin filled her face as she glided back and forth with her feet off the ground, a child's sensation of flying. She had the security she needed with her mother right there giving her little baby pushes and helping her be comfortable with this new activity. It was a delightful experience for her in learning about the world and her place in it.

I imagine that from her toddler perspective a swing could appear a bit intimidating. Most things in her life were small, sized down to fit her world. The towering structure of the swing set must have been monumental to her. And seeing other children swing high and very fast probably looked quite dangerous. With her mother at her side she felt safe to laugh and have fun. She had yet to learn the lesson of being careful when doing things such as this.

Something distracted her one time and she let go of the chains. Before her mother could catch her, she took a tumble out of the swing and got skinned up and bruised a bit. It was nothing serious to the adults who decided whether her injury needed a bandage or a trip to the hospital, but it was serious business to her. It hurt!

She made certain we all knew that for her it was a pretty traumatic event. Her mother held her and consoled her with love, cleaned her up, and wiped away the tears. Of course she was a little unsure about whether she wanted to swing again. Once she settled down from the accident, her mother persisted in getting her back on the swing, encouraging her with a nod of approval to hold on tight. And as she swung her little back-and-forths, she, too, nodded her head, repeating with her little toddler voice, "Hold on tight. Hold on tight. Hold on tight."

I am amazed by the amount of knowledge a child amasses by the time they are five or six years old. At no other time in their life will they accomplish as much as they do in these first few years. They learn to walk, run, jump, and climb. They learn to speak. They learn to read and write, and some even learn multiple languages. They begin to learn numbers, basic mathematics, and how to tell time. They are able to clothe themselves and take care of the basic responsibilities of life. Social skills are adopted. They form personalities and beliefs about who they are and how they fit in the world. Most of these beliefs carry on into adult life, dictating much of who they become and what they do.

When my granddaughter got back on the swing with her mother's gentle nudges and encouragement, she nodded and kept repeating, "Hold on tight." My thoughts, like her swing, swayed back and forth. The proud grandfather in me smiled with my heart warmed by how cute and brave she was to get back up. She was back to having fun, able to smile again with the new lesson in being careful. I was proud of her for not giving up. I was also proud of her mother's encouragement and dedication to stay with her through this learning experience, focusing on the fun and delight rather than the danger. She knew her little girl had learned her lesson. It was one of many childhood lessons in learning the element of safety when having fun.

My thoughts then swung back to wondering about the many ways I encourage myself to just cling to the chains of life and hold on tight. There were times when I chose to get back on my swing; to get back up and give it another go; to persist, learning my lesson in falling and being a little more cautious the next time. Yet my thoughts quickly fixated on the choices made in fear, in ignorance, to appease my ego, and, regrettably, as acts of revenge – when after my bumps and bruises I chose to never set foot on that playground again. So easily my thoughts went to beating myself up over the steps not taken, overshadowing the many, many times I made choices in service to myself and others. And that made me wonder why. Why is it I so easily focus on things that went wrong, regretful choices, events that did not go in my favor, or others I felt had done me wrong?

Things happen. They always do. Life has its twists and turns and times when we are tumbled out of the swing. Sometimes there is someone there to dust us off and help us back up; other times not. There are too many possibilities for all of life to go exactly as planned. We create stories about life events. Some are happy, loving, and inspirational. But the stories that seem to have the most impact on what we believe about the world and our place in it tend to be the ones that taught us to be cautious. We remember the hurt.

Think back to a time when you set out to do something and everything went awry. It could have been a project at home not going as planned, difficulties you had moving to a new city, or delays and mishaps you had on a vacation. Perhaps you can look back and laugh about it, or maybe not. Either way, it was only an experience. You made the effort and survived. If you were to tell someone the story, would it be about the dismay of everything going wrong, or would you instead share the lessons learned in making the effort? In other words, would your story be about the fall, or getting back into the swing and holding on?

Your stories stack together to form a book that becomes the operations manual for how you live. In following that manual, you make choices and take actions in compliance with instructions you know. The results created are typically in alignment with your book of life, and with each story the book continues to write itself, with new chapters being added each day.

You live by the contents of that book – by your life stories and the judgments you have made about them. Life can go on autopilot, following the messages therein. Your reaction to any event is at the mercy of the stories you make up, all following the same theme. Any event can be a trigger. Your reaction to it is evidence of the way you have reacted to prior events and your general attitude toward others. As long as the pattern persists, an opinionated story supporting the attitude you have of the world becomes engrained in your brain.

Once this behavior is established, your stories written, and your operations manual for life published, your subconscious mind seeks conditions and circumstances that support the beliefs in your manual. You get triggered; you react. That reaction is fueled by emotion. The emotional response is deemed important. The important things are categorized and filed away in your manual for future reference. It truly is a magnificent survival mechanism. Unfortunately, without guidance it can be used against you.

A different perspective on the word *react* is *to re-act*. A reaction to an event – something done or said, is a reenactment of the story already written, with the same attitude and emotions as your collected beliefs. Your reaction to an event reinforces and accelerates the emotional fuel. An actual neural pathway is being reinforced and made very efficient. Each time a similar event occurs, you call on the learned behavior more and more rapidly. When events occur that really irk you – really stir up angst, frustration, jealousy, and even hatred – they are triggers being pulled on the emotion you associate with the stories already in your book. As you continue to react in the same manner, your new stories reinforce the old. Each similar event further fuels the emotion.

The way to interrupt this pattern is to understand the difference between reacting and responding. A response to an event involves making a conscious choice to change your attitude about it. Choosing to respond takes discipline and patience. Troubling events really push our buttons, and it takes a lot of effort to respond to them appropriately rather than reacting; these are the reactions you want to hold and embrace as being the truth – anger, frustration, and feeling victimized. You want to be right and you want others to be wrong. You want to *hold on tight* so that you minimize the chance of being hurt again.

For events such as these, you need a predetermined response. And you need tools you can use when such a need arises. A simple example is getting cut off in traffic. When someone makes an aggressive move without signaling, catching you by surprise, you can get angry even if you're a very tranquil person. There is a basketful of emotional triggers being set off involving your own safety as well as that of the other driver and those around you, the damage that could ensue from an accident, and the inconsideration and impatience of the other driver. The typical reaction is to get angry and pass judgment that they are an irresponsible jerk. But you don't know their story. Perhaps there is an emergency, or they were just not paying attention at the moment. Maybe they are victim to a way of thinking that makes them feel justified in driving that way and compelled to do so. Maybe they just made a mistake. Regardless, the tool to use in such an event is to calm your reaction and choose to respond in a different manner. Accept that what they did was not safe, yet be grateful that no harm was done. And be forgiving. Allow them to be who they are with every right to have their life journey as you have to have yours.

What separates us from creatures, plants, and elements is that we have the freedom of choice and the memory of the events that created our subconscious programs. In becoming aware of these programs, you can choose your attitude and response. You are not held hostage by instinct and conditioned response. You can accept your emotional reaction to an event as being a natural form of self-protection. You can then pause, and then choose how you are going to respond. It takes practice and discipline to interrupt your natural reaction. But in time you will master using this tool when events happen that stir your emotions.

Using the tool of responding appropriately instead of reacting teaches us responsibility – *the ability to respond*. When my granddaughter fell out of the swing, she cried. It's what toddlers do to get attention. She had learned to let a grownup know when something hurt so the grownup could fix it or at least comfort her with attention. It formed one of her first stories and beliefs. She learned to be responsible for her own safety while on a swing. Had she refused to get back up it would have been her emotional reaction making that choice. And without her mother's encouragement, she probably would have let that choice prevail.

Such events establish how we think, behave, act, and make the choices that form our lives. When we simply react to the emotion we feel, we reinforce the belief that roused it, and it becomes habitual behavior. What undesirable results do we create along the way to avoid falling and getting bruised again? How many of us cling to the chains of life and repeat, "Hold on tight"?

There is a cycle to learned behavior. I touched on this cycle earlier when writing about how we establish our comfort zone. It starts with the core values we adopt as small children – good and bad, right and wrong – which we use to assign meaning to our experiences and form beliefs about who we are that drive our thoughts and thinking.

We learn to let our subconscious mind take over our day-to-day activities. We delegate more and more tasks to the subconscious so that we don't have to think about every choice every minute of the day. Take, for example, driving a car. Have you ever reached your destination and realized you remember little of the drive to get there? All the while you were operating the gas and brake pedals, maybe the clutch and gearshift. You were steering, using turn signals, watching the mirrors. Maybe you were adjusting the heat or air conditioning, and changing the channel on the radio. You watched out for cars and trucks hurtling at you at very close distances, their drivers ironically on autopilot themselves! And yet you remember very little of this. You passed off your driving skills to your subconscious to handle, freeing up your mind to think about other things: the grocery list, the call you need to return, the fuel gauge getting a little low, and preparing for the meeting you have two days from now.

Your subconscious mind works every minute of every day. It does not sleep. It does not take holidays or have weekends off. It is constantly attending to the tasks you give it. Once given a task it always performs as instructed. It does not argue, question, or refuse any instruction given. It does as it is told to do every time a task is presented. That is why you do not remember driving your car. You didn't have to drive it. It is as if someone else drove.

The same holds true for almost every event you experience. By the time you are a young adult you have experienced almost everything you will ever encounter in life. Fewer and fewer events come up that you have not in some way experienced before. Based on the beliefs you have about you and your world, you make choices regarding how to handle each, and then for the most part delegate that responsibility to subconscious thought. There is a point after which life is mostly a repeating cycle of events and unconsciously reacting to them.

Subconscious thought creates automatic behavior – your attitude, your mannerisms, and the choices you make each day without thinking about them. You *hold on tight* to what you believe to be true about your world and how you fit in. You have learned behavior that you feel is essential to your survival, keeping you safe and out of danger's way. The choices you make and your feelings about them are based on this automatic behavior. The results you get from your choices provide feedback that supports the belief that started it all.

When the results you get from the choices you make support what you believe to be true, you are in your comfort zone. Your belief about who you are and what it takes to be safe and secure has been reinforced. Your subconscious mind has done its task and is satisfied the work is complete. The cycle continues, building the belief until it becomes your default way of thinking, feeling, and operating. The swing of life goes on. Hold on tight.

Change Your Story

The only limits for tomorrow are the doubts we have today.
— Pittacus Lore

In the previous chapter I mentioned that we create an operations manual for how to go about our day-to-day business. Events happen and we react in accordance with the manual. Results pretty much follow the book, and with each event a new story is created. Chapters continue to be added and the book grows into volumes. Certainly our lives should diverge from the story as we learn and grow, yet the story seems to flow with very few radical changes, if any.

Imagine that book being rewritten as a screenplay, and a movie of your life is filmed. The characters have specific roles they are to play. The story is either a good one or a bad one. It is influenced by scenes that preceded it, and further influences scripts that follow. Your "life movie" supports what you believe about the world and those around you. As events happen you place them into your movie in such a way that the plot line continues to make sense. The cast members are the perfect choices to support the story, and they play their parts very well. Circumstances occur that form the perfect movie set for recording the film. The story supports what you believe about the world and those around you at the time the event happened. This is true whether you are living an uplifting, inspirational life or a sad drama full of disappointment and despair.

It is interesting to reflect on your cast members and their roles. They are each acting out their life movie as well, and you are a cast member in their film. You go about your business unaware of the role you are playing in their movie. And it doesn't matter what your role is. They cast you in it because you are the perfect fit for their script. You unknowingly perform your lines and actions as a perfect fit for the story they are living.

Likewise, the cast members of your movie are just living their lives doing what they normally do. They are not performing or acting off a specific script. You did not have to hold auditions to decide who would play the lead and supporting roles. They are in your life movie because the lines they speak and their actions fit into your story. You do your best to direct them, but others do what they do because they are living out their life movies just as you are living out yours. We all wish we could have played out certain scenes in our past differently or made different choices, or that our cast members would have acted differently.

It is well accepted that we cannot change the past. Events that have happened cannot be changed without the use of a time machine. Even if we could conjure up some science-fiction magic to go back and change events, the results would most likely be the same. People did what they did, and said what they said. The weather was what it was. The sun came up in the east and set in the west. The events happened and there is no changing that.

So the question becomes why anybody would want to change the timeline. It is because you had an emotional reaction to an event that wrote another scene in your life movie. You might want to make different choices, say something different in an argument, get revenge, or prevent the event that warrants revenge. You want to remove an undesirable scene from the movie, for it is that script that seems to influence the story that follows and the drama that continues.

Though events and facts of the past cannot be changed, your emotional reaction to them can be changed. The way you interpret what happened, what was said, or what was done can be changed at any moment. It is your interpretation of the facts that makes up the story line. It can be changed at any time. To change your life, change your story about all the events that have led up to now. This can be difficult to accept and embrace. We tend to hold fast to our stories because they are all we know. When things happen, we cast judgment on what they mean. We make up a story.

Revisit the events of the past from a different perspective. Of course, rewriting the past isn't easy because your movie is programmed to play one and only one way. It takes a conscious effort to alter your perception of those events and their influence on your story line. It takes effort to accept the events for what they were and invent the story that comes from them.

Many of your stories began in your childhood. Sometimes events happened that violated your core values about what is good and what is bad. When something "bad" happened, a plot line was formed. Then other events conformed to the plot line so that it continued to flow and make sense. Beliefs began to form and create subconscious thought that now drives your emotions, your attitude, the choices you make, and the ensuing results. The results follow the story line well and further reinforce the beliefs that started it all.

It is easy to fall victim to this cycle. By being a victim to the cycle, life is predictable. You function as well as you can. You continue to think in the same manner, react as you always have, and make choices that are comfortable. In other words, you live in your comfort zone, even if you hate it. Following the story line you created from past events takes little conscious effort.

The most influential events usually involve other people in your life. There is something they said, did, or did not say or do when they should have. Based on the stories you had embraced until that point in time, you cast judgment on them as though you were watching the movie play out as expected. Their violation was recorded as such, and you hold this to be true about their character. In this way you form general judgments about who is to be trusted and whom not to trust.

There were "good" things that happened, too, and they also influenced the story you created; however, it was the "bad" experiences that influenced your protective behavior to avoid getting hurt again. The events have already taken place. There is no need to create an artificial scenario to avoid them happening again. Remember the genie who brings forth the people and conditions that support what you are thinking about. There is no need for the drama of the past to continue. At any moment the movie can be paused, rewound, and played differently. The cast of characters can be given different scripts and you can be given a new directive in the film, one of fulfillment, hope, prosperity, and happiness. An entirely different script can be written off the same events and the new script used to influence the scenes that are to follow. You write the script for your life movie. The cast of characters follows that script. You can apply a new script to past events and come up with a new movie at any time. You have the power and the right to create a life you love to live. And you deserve it from this point forward.

Changing the story line is uncomfortable. When confronted with a situation in which a reenactment of the same story is about to occur, you can make a conscious choice to look at the event from a different perspective. To do so is off script. It takes courage to change the belief system that you have forged over time. It takes courage to pick up the remote, press the pause button, and choose to respond rather than react. Rather than be a victim of the drama, choose not to include the situation in the same old movie. It is not necessary to know why it happened. All that is needed is to accept it as an event independent of the new life story you wish to create. Past events occurred because of choices you made in accordance with the ongoing script that led up to now. The story around them does not need be carried forward. Failures can be reshaped as learning opportunities, hurt turned to compassion, and injustice used as the fuel to peacefully confront the improprieties against you and others.

Another thing to contemplate in changing your life story is a concept that is difficult to grasp from the perspective of your life story: Nothing is good or bad; your mind makes it so. No matter what is happening in your life, your mind decides whether it is good or bad. From others being a little rude or inconsiderate, to the greatest atrocities of humankind, you decide whether it is good or bad. Your story sprouted from your core values, so it is you who ultimately decides whether its chapters are good or bad.

This is certainly not to imply that injustice to others is not bad. There is certainly a distinction between that which is moral and that which is evil. We share a common belief that we each have the right to live. We have the right to love. We have the right to persevere. When there is an atrocity that is denying someone of those rights, we deem this bad. And that's a good thing. It is our minds that make it so.

If there were difficult times in your life or despicable things that happened to you that caused you to struggle with your story, it is okay to deem them as bad things that happened. More than likely they involved another person or a group of people. I personally have found it quite difficult to let go and change my story about those who did me wrong. I have come to accept that what happened is done. Yes, it hurt, but it does not have to dictate how I live my life today. Nor does it yours. In changing your story, there is an uncomfortable exercise of forgiveness and acceptance. To forgive is to release someone from responsibility for how you feel. Unfortunately they were living out their life story and your paths crossed. I am of the belief that most people are good, moral people, and that they have good intentions. Sometimes they make horrible choices. And when they make them, they do not fully understand why; they are just operating under the programmed life story they know. Releasing them of responsibility for how you feel places the responsibility back where it belongs: It is you and only you who is responsible for your feelings. And it is those feelings that support the life story you are creating. To change your life story, take full responsibility for it.

The point of decision lies in the now. Your new perspective will not change something that already happened, and it is not to be applied to something that will happen in the future. It is a conscious choice to revisit and change your *interpretation* of the past – now. It is a choice about how to fit the events taking place now into the life story you wish to live now. There is no reason to worry about what is going to happen tomorrow. Follow the recipe I laid out earlier, know what you want, believe you can have it, trust that all will work out, and do something. Check on the results you are getting and how you feel about them. Change something if you need to. All you have is now; it is your point of power. You rewrite your life movie from where you have been to where you are going through your attitude and the choices you make today.

What Is in the Way?

I've missed more than 9,000 shots in my career. I've lost almost 300 games. Twenty-six times I've been trusted to take the game-winning shot and missed. I've failed over and over and over again in my life. And that is why I succeed.
– Michael Jordan

Imagine being involved in a sports team, perhaps as a player or the parent of a player; or maybe someone you dearly care for is playing. The team has spent several months organizing, getting coaches to help out, and practicing drills and techniques of the game. You have studied others who have mastered the game, forming strategies for scoring and winning. You have put together plays for offense and defense so that all members of the team know what they need to do, and when. You have your uniforms and a team logo. You are feeling pretty good about the team and are ready to play.

It is now game day. Your team steps out onto the field to get warmed up. Your opponent takes their place on the field as well. You cannot help but notice that they don't know the game well. They don't have enough players to fill the roster. They look inept, showing little skill. It is obvious that it is going to be a rout – an easy win. When the game begins, your team easily scores, and continues scoring. Soon the thrill of the imminent victory shallows. There is no challenge. Wouldn't you have instead preferred an opponent that was as good as your team, or maybe even a tad bit better to force you to play your best game?

It is not that we do not care for things coming easily; it's simply that in the realm of growth we know we learn best from being challenged. In a challenge there is an emotional charge, and it is in that charge of emotion that learning occurs. So whether it's a game of sports or avoiding the chocolate cake being offered, there is an emotional charge in both victory and defeat. It is this emotional charge that sets the stage for future behavior.

What stands between you and what you want? Who is your opponent? When pursuing a goal, liken it to a sports team that is up against a formidable opponent. The other team is your default way of thinking, feeling, and acting. It is the result of prior emotional charges from events and how you experienced them. This team formed over time. When setting a goal to accomplish something never done before, you are up against this foe. And they are good – very good.

WHAT IS IN THE WAY?

What is interesting is that this opposing team has spies. It has infiltrated the ranks and knows your every move. It knows your strategies. It knows your weaknesses. It knows how to counter every attempt you make at scoring. It constantly tricks you into going back to your old way of doing things. In other words, it encourages you to give up and accept defeat. The only way you can score on this foe is with a clear intention and determination to do so. Remember the recipe? Know what you want. Believe you can have it. Trust it will all work out. And do something. Continually combining those ingredients eventually results in a play that will beat this sly challenger.

The mind is a manifesting tool. Everything in existence created by humans was first in someone's mind as an idea. There has been much study in the quantum physics world of the effect thought has on matter. What we think about gets created. However, this is not to say that every thought immediately turns into something. If we could immediately think things into existence, life would be chaos with houses, cars, boats, relationships, babies, and businesses popping up like the lights on a pinball machine.

There are two reasons why things don't just pop into existence. First, there is an incubation period to test whether or not the intended thought is worthy of coming into being. Since birth, your mind has been busy putting together neural pathways that form your way of thinking. This is what you have learned. The big lessons in life came with a strong dose of emotion, and if you are like most, this emotional charge was unpleasant. In your interpretations of these "bad" events your mind formed a fabulous way to protect you from danger. Through the desire to learn and interact safely with your environment, the thoughts produced by your neural web are directed outward as your behavior – your personality. They dictate your actions and lead you to make choices and decisions that support what you believe. Your personality radiates out and attracts the people and events that fit.

What does this all mean? Simply put, if you think things will go wrong, they do. If you are optimistic they will work out, they do. What you think ultimately manifests into existence to validate and reinforce your beliefs. Yet it does not happen instantly. This manifestation requires an incubation period. If you recall from an earlier chapter, there is a metaphysical defense against change. It pushes back. It has already installed the mental program that tells you you cannot have what you want and why you don't deserve it. Only a sustained vision and belief that you will create what you desire can get you through the incubation period and bring your vision to fruition.

It is actually possible to think a different life into existence. The only reason you struggle in making changes is that you are not willing to do what's uncomfortable in training your mind to think in a different way. Your default way of thinking is out to sabotage you. Your mind formed your neural net to protect you, so thinking in a different way is a threat. *That threat is what is in the way.* It is a very natural defense mechanism.

The other reason thoughts don't just pop into existence is because we are all energetically connected. We share a collective consciousness. As we set our intention and choose to

WHAT IS IN THE WAY?

think, act, and react in a different way, so are others. It takes a little time for the manifestation of creation to come together in consensus. However, you can get priority treatment. This magical power that comes into play – the genie who grants your wishes – pays attention to what you want and to your resolute intention to get it. Just as with getting through the incubation period of manifestation, getting the attention of this omnipotent force requires that you have a sustained vision and the belief to create what it is you desire. Have you ever had an idea and out of nowhere someone else came up with the same idea? It is almost as though they broke into your brain and stole it. I truly believe that thoughts go out into this collective consciousness, are processed and refined, then ideas and solutions are transmitted back. Those tuned in to the frequency receive the idea as a "eureka!" moment. The one who has clearest intention and takes immediate action on the idea is usually the one credited for it.

Similar to the chapter "What Is Uncomfortable," the title of this chapter, "What Is in the Way?" is as much a statement as it is a question. When you pursue a new idea or just want to change something you don't like in your life, there's a good likelihood you will be met with obstacles. Asking yourself "What is in the way?" directs you to the obstacles you create in your mind that keep you from your dreams. Your obstacles are your gifts. They identify your programs – the stories you made up from your reactions to past events. In identifying these programs, each can be assessed as to whether it is working for you or against you.

For example, I have a program I created as a young child that gets triggered now and then. Early on I had some respiratory problems that limited my activity. I couldn't run as fast or as far as the other kids. I also have an odd eye that does not behave as it should. I have some problems with depth perception that have kept me away from most sports – nothing terribly serious, yet I stood out as being inferior as a child. I was often bullied. I was one of the last to be chosen on the team, and was ignored by the elite crowd. It was difficult to know who was truly a friend. I was so frustrated and felt victimized. It stirred much anger in me and I adopted an "us and them" belief, complete with programmed reactions. There were those of "us" who belonged together, and "them" who were out to get us.

It is almost silly and embarrassing to admit this as an adult, and just as embarrassing to admit that it still comes out from time to time, because when it does, everything seems to be an uphill battle. I do not get cooperation from others. I get down and feel as though I have no support. As soon as I recognize this old program is running, I accept it as a part of me, and then remember that I do not have to operate as though there is an "us" and a "them." Instead, there is only "all of us *and* them." I have a choice to be compassionate toward others, accepting them for who they are and the gifts they have to offer. I make this shift whenever this old program is triggered. Both programs are based on the same childhood events: to be a victim or to remember the importance of accepting others for who they are and showing empathy. I now recognize *what is in the way* when I feel victimized,

WHAT IS IN THE WAY?

down on myself, and without support. And I have the gift of choice to respond as I desire, loving and caring.

The programs will always exist; this is how we operate. They can be activated at any time, either voluntarily or automatically. When automatically activated and working against you, you need tools to respond in a new way. The obstacles are there for a reason. If nothing else, they keep things from popping in and out of existence and creating chaos. When confronted with a challenge – the opposing team spying on your every move – you have the opportunity to exercise the discipline of getting clear about what you want and maintaining sustained focus on it. Take time to assess what is in your way. What repeating patterns of reaction and results challenge you? For example, what emotions are stirred in you by common events like traffic, crowds, and people not paying attention to what they are doing? This is evidence of how you have programmed yourself to operate. And only you can eject the program and install another.

It begins with asking yourself, "What is in the way?" Think back on your life to when the programs were installed. The obstacles you encounter are from the old programs that are running your show. Once you recognize them you have the chance to do the uncomfortable work of writing a new program that you can call on when the old one is triggered. It does not happen overnight. It takes time to recognize the old patterns and the results you are creating. In time you will learn new ways to respond. Along the way you might take a few shots and miss. Eventually you will find that you can change your attitude, make new choices, and get the results you want. You will automatically delegate this new behavior to your subconscious mind, forming a new program that becomes as powerful and proficient in creating the life you want as the old one was at creating what was in the way.

Step into the Zone

*Due to circumstances beyond my control,
I am master of my fate and captain of my soul.*
– Ashleigh Brilliant

The Uncomfortable Zone is created when desire meets the doubt it is possible. The stronger the belief that it is not possible, the more uncomfortable the zone. The thought of making a change for the better stirs the emotions that create the obstacles of the mind. The emotions you feel are reflections of what you believe about yourself and the world in which you live. When there is something you want but you feel it's out of reach, you have just stepped up to your zone.

Many years ago I sought advice from an elder sage about feeling lost and without direction in my life. For a while it seemed as though he was ignoring me. His head was down, motionless, and he didn't show any signs of being interested in anything I said. He almost appeared to be asleep. Suddenly he perked up, eyes wide, looking deeply into mine. He had been listening to every word I said. I had to ask what it was that awakened his attention. It was when I said "but." It is a very powerful word when doubting you will ever have something you want. It cancels everything in front of it and is followed by the truth – your truth. And it was only my truth he was interested in talking about.

Most of my life had been a clockwork of pursuing dreams, some realized and many not. There were many years of being busy with the tick-tock of activities that made up my life: getting up in the morning, getting into a routine, doing stuff, and retiring at the end of the day, only to repeat it the next day. For most of the days of my life, not much happened. I knew the importance of being positive, setting goals, and pursuing them with confidence and the belief that they were possible to achieve. I knew that I needed to be crystal clear on my intentions and commit to them. I knew that my state of mind was paramount and that my attitude was more important than any skill or innate ability I possessed. Having the discipline to manage my thoughts and activities was the key to a happy life.

Yet something was missing. I did not feel that I was serving my full purpose. Granted, I was doing well with my family and in my job, and generally had a pretty good life. I just felt that I was not doing what I was supposed to do. And each time I had a thought of doing something else, I followed it with the ever-so-powerful word "but." I would sometimes wonder what I could have accomplished had I pursued any number of my dreams and desires. Where would I be today if I had known then what I know now? I now know that when that haunting thought arises, I simply accept that I would not be where I am today, enjoying the wonderful life I live, without those experiences.

When you speak of the things you would like, the places you wish to go, and the life you want, do you then follow it with the word "but" and the reason (or reasons) why it is difficult? *But* marks the boundary of your Uncomfortable Zone. And it lights the path to the choices you need to make to get what you want. To take that step in, to do what is uncomfortable and perhaps frightening, you must learn to accept and challenge your truth. It is what you believe to be true about yourself and the world around you, and you have naturally formed that truth over time from your brain working exactly as it should to keep you safe and out of harm's way. Sometimes these programs are overly protective and get in the way.

It is at this point, when you stop yourself from pursuing your dreams, that you can identify where you need to do your work. Is it a limited vision? Self-doubt? Lack of faith? Things you do to avoid getting hurt? What is keeping you from getting up and doing something that could move you forward? Something is triggering your programs to be cautious and wary of making a change. When you feel that doubt – worrying about what could happen, and feel the fear of doing something new, you must decide whether it is real or based on events that have long gone by.

THE UNCOMFORTABLE ZONE

Reflect deeply and look for those reasons you feel you cannot go after your dreams. You may find they follow a pattern, and that hesitation shows up in most everything you do. Perhaps you procrastinate in taking action; or you do 90 percent of the work and then stop. It could be that you are worried about what others will think. Is it indecision, self-doubt, or even guilt? There are many things you can discover about yourself when you examine the words that follow "but." It takes humility and discipline to look back on your life and ask why it is you cannot do the things you need to be doing. What stories have you been making up about yourself and others? Because if you continue to follow those story lines, you will continue to make the same choices.

What are the prices you pay for your choices? What costs are others incurring for your choices? Even though the answers have profound consequences, they are elusive and require contemplation. Because there are not definitive prices for your decisions, you don't give the cost much weight when you make a decision. You can go on living each day much like the past, feeling it doesn't matter much. Each time you think it's okay to make the same choices today and make up for them tomorrow, a little amount is added to this debt. It is only over time that you realize the cost of a selfish choice. This is normal.

There are characteristics we admire in others – honesty, integrity, generosity, loyalty, dependability, and kindness; and those we wish to avoid – selfishness, jealousy, vengefulness, deceitfulness, and being manipulative; and both kinds of characteristics exist in all of us. But this is only your *behavior*; it is not you. Your behavior is the outcome of your programs. It is simply your automatic way to avoid getting hurt, even when the threat is imaginary. You can adopt a new perspective toward others and toward life, but inside you know you are the same person choosing to respond from rational choice rather than react from automatic programs.

Making a change is uncomfortable. It is uncomfortable because it challenges the way you think. The way you think got you to where you are today, and you take some level of pride in who you are and what you have accomplished. To challenge that is to challenge your sense of self-worth. *Will I still be happy and satisfied if I make this change? Will I fail? What will others think? Will they still love me?* Changing threatens who you are and how you fit in your world, which is quite frightening deep within, whether you are willing to admit it or not. It creates a great discomfort that must be overcome if you want to see that change.

To step up to the Uncomfortable Zone, face the fear, and push forth is an act of courage, but even more it is an attitude and a state of being. Setting an intention and acting on it in an effective and responsible way is taking a step into the zone. Do it with grace and confidence. Be aware of warning signs along the way. Sometimes it is difficult to discern whether an obstacle should be overcome or is an indication that you are not on the correct path. Be flexible and agile so you can adjust your path as you see fit. Keep forging forward with confidence and the willingness to learn from your mistakes.

There will be victories and times of celebration for goals achieved. Some of your accomplishments might not seem significant at the time; later you may come to realize the worth of what you accomplished. You might give up on a particular goal and feel like you failed, but remember to simply change your perspective from failure to that of a learning experience. It is not that you failed; you just tried something that didn't work out as planned.

There is no divine proclamation that dooms some people to fail while others succeed. Those who get what they desire are not blessed in a special way. They do not have special skills or innate talent. And those who live in frustration, feeling trapped and denied a better life, are not fated to a life of bad luck. It is not because they are inadequate in any way. It is not a divine force conspiring against them. It is being unwilling to challenge what they believe to be true and make different choices.

Look at the results in your life and see what you can do better. Strive to improve. Evaluate where you are and where you are going. Use as your compass your core values – those that guide you as to what is right and what is wrong. Things are either going your way or they are not. You are either satisfied or you desire something better. Always ask yourself why: "Why is making a change so important; why is it no longer acceptable to keep doing what I have been doing?" Focus on the reasons why you must do the uncomfortable and inconvenient things. Your reasons provide the directions you must take. Use these signs as guides to a fulfilled life. To avoid the discomfort is to avoid making a change.

Making different choices and acting on them requires a change of attitude. Your attitude shows others how you feel about yourself and the world. The best way to improve your attitude is to smile. Look in the mirror. Smile big. It is very therapeutic and immediately lifts your spirits and helps instill a feeling of power. Smile often. You will find it is contagious. Others will smile back. You will find others more cooperative and willing to work with you, and for you.

Don't complain. Focus on the facts and not on the story behind them – yours or anyone else's. Complaining concentrates your focus on the things you do not like. A message is sent to your subconscious mind and reinforces the programs you already have in place that are not working for you. Always look for the benefits in the choices you make. They can be obscure, as in a lesson being learned. And they might not show themselves for some time, so add patience to your new attitude.

Accept that most people have good intentions and that they care for others. Like you, they sometimes make mistakes. They are sometimes inconsiderate, greedy, jealous, and insensitive. This does not make them bad people. Just as you would not want the responsibility of never making a mistake, so it goes for others. They are just playing out their own stories and probably do not even know they are doing it. Blaming others for your discouragement is avoiding responsibility for yourself; however, it is not the same as being irresponsible – it is just succumbing to a default way of thinking that you have developed over time.

Associate with people who think the way you wish to think. Do what you can to study how the mind works to better understand yourself, how you think, how you react, where your attitude comes from, and the choices you make. Consider your results, everything around you, and the connections you have with others. This is the compelling evidence for what you believe and how you live your life.

Take ownership and responsibility for all results you create. Take ownership of your part in what is happening now. If you feel violated, remember that you made a series of choices that brought you to the situation you are in. What is happening in your life is a reflection of your beliefs and evidence of what you think. Embrace the emotion of accepting what is. Be inquisitive about why you feel the way you do and whether or not it is important to feel that way. What is most important is how you are going to feel tomorrow about the choices you made today.

As I mentioned at the outset of *The Uncomfortable Zone*, I am a personal-development record. I have read, given away, repurchased, and redonated racks of self-help books. I have traveled afar, investing significant amounts of time and money to learn from the sages of success and happiness. I've listened repeatedly to countless vinyl records, cassette tapes, CDs, and online courses and podcasts. I've associated myself with positive people and those who believe in personal development. I've studied the topic my whole life, even when I was a child and my mother shared her belief that the only constraints to life lie in the mind, providing me a foundation on which to build positive thinking. I can recite many personal-development quotes and the essence of countless teachings. It has been a life-long quest to find satisfaction. Yet it was not until quite later in my adulthood that any of this began to take hold. The studies, the work, the lectures were all for naught until I learned something quite simple in applying this knowledge: Instead of striving for success in order to be fulfilled and content, I should strive to be fulfilled and content each day, and in so doing unexpectedly experience success.

The Uncomfortable Zone concept was birthed from asking myself why, after years of studying and applying personal-development skills, I still wasn't living a fulfilled life. On the steps of the courthouse on that brisk autumn day of my bankruptcy many years ago, I consciously asked, "Now what?" There were some underlying thoughts and beliefs in play as well. The full dialogue was in essence: "I know what it takes to be successful. I have been doing the work. And now I am here, broke and deflated. Obviously I am doing something wrong. Now what?"

Initially I felt very despondent about being bankrupt. I cursed. I cried. I slammed my fists into my pillow. In the privacy of my home, I let it out and allowed myself to get through it. I drained myself to the point of feeling nothing. Then I accepted that if something was going to change, I needed to change the way I thought. That conjured up a whole new set of feelings: how would I know what to fix if I didn't know what was broken? This led to the "aha" realization that in seeking what was wrong I was showing others that I was broken or flawed in some way.

The profound realization that the life I was living was the direct result of choices I had made might have come from a book, an inspirational movie, or something someone said. More important, this realization was evidence that I was in perfect working order. If I could create a life of being broke and down on my luck, the same effort could create a life of prosperity and fulfillment.

The lessons I learned by forging ahead and staying true to my vision are in this book. My years of study had already provided the recipe of life, and the original idea for the book was based on the recipe alone. Yet I knew there was something more. I found that even though I had mastered the ingredients of the recipe long ago, it wasn't working for me because I wasn't combining them properly. And checking for doneness – paying attention to what was happening and how I felt about it – was the instruction I had been overlooking.

I encourage you to accept yourself for who you are: perfect and capable of succeeding at anything you choose to pursue. Learn what you believe about yourself and the world around you. Pay attention to how you react to events and people. This helps you understand how you think and what you believe. Unearth how that affects your unconscious thought – your autopilot.

Success is not an elusive brass ring on the carousel of life; so simply hoping that the ring comes within reach is a futile desire. Stretch out to reach it, and do not let fear or pride deter you. If things are going well, great! Keep doing them. If there is something you wish to change, follow the recipe: know what you want, believe you can have it, trust it will all work out, and do something; combine the ingredients evenly, consistently, and repeatedly; and check for doneness. Allow yourself to make mistakes. If you encounter obstacles along the way, figure out why you put them there. And most of all, if it feels uncomfortable, know that you are at the boundary where many turn away in fear. When you step up to the zone, examine why it is you fear taking that next step. Learn about your behavior. Challenge what you are thinking. Be grateful that a change for the better is about to take place. Then step in! The life you desire is on the other side.

Acknowledgments

I would like to first give thanks to the many who have appreciated my teachings and encouraged me in the completion of this book. I had the concepts in my mind for years and did not fully appreciate the dedication and discipline it would take to get it done, so thanks to all of you who asked the simple yet irritating question, "How's your book going?" You were the fuel that kept my engine running.

Special thanks go out to Christine Kloser, Carrie Jareed, Jean Merrill, and the rest of the Capucia team whose expert coaching brought the message of this book forth. The Get Your Book Done® and My Time to Write programs created results for me as they have for so many other authors. And thanks to my editor, Gwen Hoffnagle, who took the very rough clay of my first draft, molded it, remolded it, and re-remolded it into a final manuscript.

Thanks go out to my community of PSI Seminars graduates for the encouragement to help me recognize, with love and respect, my own programs that got in the way of living the life I now enjoy.

And thanks to my family for the parts they did not even know they were playing: To my late father, Russ, for the path of learning I followed and the lessons therein. To my mother, Aline, for giving me all I needed to know at a very young age and for her patience in my taking so long to live it. To my brothers, Charles, Curtis, and Chad, whom I admire and am in awe of for their genius and artistic talent. To my children – Stephanie, for her gentle sweetness and dedication to everything she does; Kristen, for her delightful humor and being a Super Mom; and Mikey, from whom I learn to be outward-focused, fair, and flexible, and to have fun.

About the Author

Don Awalt has enjoyed a variety of educational accomplishments that include a formal degree in business/accounting from Colorado State University and working as a business analyst for a software application that specialized in construction job cost accounting. On the other end of the spectrum he is a lifelong performing musician with experience wearing a tuxedo and performing with an orchestra, and wearing spandex in the eighties playing rock and pop in dance bars until 2:00AM. His informal education is from SHKU, the School of Hard Knocks University, from which he holds many advanced degrees, and from which graduates have the privilege and honor to use the same acronym for the School of Handy Knowledge University if and when they so desire.

In Don's journey to figure out what life is really about, he found the Lakota way of life to be quite intriguing and in alignment with his spiritual beliefs. He has crawled into countless sweat lodges to pray, give thanks, and ask for guidance in his life. He has sat at the drum in many Sundance ceremonies to sing-in and celebrate another year of humans coexisting with the rest of creation.

One very uncomfortable change Don made in his life, and which provided much of the inspiration for this book, was to open up, let the world know of his multifaceted life, and not be concerned about what others thought. He discovered there were many who were inspired and intrigued by his diverse experiences once he made the awkward choice to be open and authentic and to live his truth.

Don is the proud father of three adult children whom he admires and thanks for the many lessons they taught him and the examples they set each day to make the world a better place.

www.ingramcontent.com/pod-product-compliance
Lightning Source LLC
Chambersburg PA
CBHW052139110526
44591CB00012B/1781